Super
salads

More than 200 fresh
and delicious recipes for
every day and all seasons

Super
salads

Reader's
Digest

Published by The Reader's Digest Association Limited
Sydney • London • New York • Montreal

Introduction

Salads are for all seasons. Year—round, there's a great variety of fresh vegetables and salad greens available. Putting together combinations of flavours, colours and textures that taste delicious, look attractive and are good for you is a surprisingly easy and rewarding way to eat. When making salads, you can travel the world. Many countries have their own signature salad dishes that highlight certain salad greens, herbs or other seasonings. Some include rice, pasta, beans or grains for carbohydrate and protein while others use bread as a way to make a little go a long way.

This collection of more than 200 recipes includes classic salads such as Waldorf and salade Niçoise as well as modern ideas for low-cost family meals and luxurious dishes for special occasions. There are main-course and side-dish recipes for meat, seafood and poultry lovers as well as many vegetarian options. For a sweet finale, dessert fruit salads are the perfect showcase for top-quality seasonal produce.

We hope that you enjoy using these recipes and are inspired to create some of your own. And, if you're in a hurry, don't forget that a salad is fast food at its very best!

The Editors

Contents

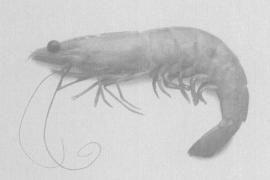

The Art of Making Salads

Salads are one of the easiest forms of cooking and basic skills are all you need. One of the keys to a great salad is to use top-quality ingredients. Here, you'll find out more about the many salad ingredients and seasonings now available and the benefits for both your palate and your health.

Salad days

Salad making is one of the easiest forms of meal preparation and one of the most versatile. It provides scope for a great deal of creativity and imagination, drawing on a wide range of ingredients. Gone are the days when a salad was little more than an afterthought, a plain little affair comprised of a few sad lettuce leaves, bottled beetroot, a sliced tomato and a dollop of salad cream. Today's salads are full of flavour and beneficial nutrients.

reap the benefits

A salad that you've made yourself has the great advantage in that you know exactly what's in it, right down to the last grain of salt. Salad greens, raw or cooked vegetables, crunchy grains, different types of pasta, fresh berries, citrus fruits, hard-boiled eggs, nuts, rice, soft and hard cheeses, meat, poultry and fresh or canned fish – you can draw on all these to make a salad. A flavoursome dressing provides the perfect finishing touch. This could be as simple as a mixture of good-quality olive oil and balsamic vinegar or as sophisticated as a rich cheese dressing made with Roquefort or dolcelatte. Current health recommendations include at least five servings of vegetables and fruit each day to provide a wide range of the nutrients required for general health. Regularly incorporating salads into your diet is a simple way to achieve that goal and to obtain sufficient vitamins, phytochemicals, fibre and minerals. The ideal is to choose servings according to the 'traffic light' principle. What this means in practice is that every day you should eat at least one serving of red fruit or vegetables (such as peppers, radishes, tomatoes and strawberries), at least one of yellow or orange (carrots, butternut squash or pumpkin, melon, pineapple or oranges), as well as at least one of green (broccoli, beans, courgettes, spinach, salad greens, peas, watercress, apples, pears or kiwifruit). Follow this formula and you can include the broadest possible range of nutrients in your diet in the simplest way.

eat your greens...they're good for you

✳ Some types of lettuces and other salad greens contain beta carotene, folate, vitamin C, iron and potassium. Dark green or other deeply coloured leaves have more beta carotene and vitamin C than pale ones. Cos lettuce has five times as much vitamin C and more beta carotene and folate than iceberg.

✳ Deeply coloured lettuces and greens are also high in bioflavonoids, plant pigments that are known to work with vitamin C to prevent cancer-causing cell damage.

✳ Rocket, a member of the same plant family as broccoli, is one of the most nutritious of all salad greens, with more calcium than most other varieties.

Buying equipment

A sharp knife, a chopping board, a large strainer and a bowl: everyone has the basic equipment to make a simple salad. But if you make salads often and value variety, you'll want to acquire more utensils. First on the list should be a salad spinner, which makes drying washed salad greens a quick and easy task. But whether you buy a mandoline, an eggslice or a mezzaluna for chopping herbs, always buy the best quality you can afford. Your reward will be a product that's made to last and is a pleasure to use.

for cutting & cleaning

Mandoline slicer (1) is perfect for cutting firm vegetables such as carrots into even slices. It is also useful for grating cabbage leaves finely for coleslaw. Some have multiple blades of different widths. **Mezzaluna** (2) has a sharp, curved blade for finely chopping fresh herbs. Its name means half-moon in Italian. **Vegetable brush** (3) is useful for cleaning vegetables such as mushrooms that do not need washing but do have some surface dirt that requires gentle removal. **Fruit zester** (4) makes it easy to pare very fine strips of peel from citrus fruits.

for shaping, pitting & slicing

Melon baller (1) is useful for scooping even rounds from melons or other soft fruit. **Eggslice** (2) cuts hard-boiled eggs, cooked potatoes, mushrooms, mozzarella and other firm to soft ingredients into even slices. **Cherry stoner** (3) makes the removal of cherry and olive pits easy. **Vegetable peelers** (4) come in numerous different styles, all equally efficient. Choose the type that fits most comfortably in the palm of your hand. Apart from using them to peel fruit or vegetables, vegetable peelers are good for shaving thin slices or curls from hard cheeses, vegetables and chocolate.

The nature of herbs

A handful of finely chopped fresh parsley, a tablespoon of chopped chives or a scattering of tarragon leaves gives salads an extra layer of flavour. Ideally, use fresh herbs in salads. They're best purchased as and when needed because they do not keep well for more than a few days, or, if you have the space, it's very rewarding to grow your own. Dried herbs have a stronger flavour than fresh so use them more sparingly.

1 basil

Basil is synonymous with Mediterranean cooking. Sweet basil, the most commonly used, has a warm, aniseed flavour that complements tomatoes. Thai and purple Greek basil are more pungent. Basil goes well with fish and seafood salads and pasta and rice salads. It is used to make pesto, which in turn can be used in salad dressings.

2 chives

Chives are the mildest member of the onion family. They are often used in salads, particularly ones containing hard-boiled eggs or potatoes. They team well with other herbs such as parsley, dill or chervil (which has a subtle parsley/aniseed flavour).

3 coriander

This is a love-it-or-hate-it herb with an assertive taste that contains an undercurrent of heat. It is often used with other strongly flavoured ingredients which can stand up to it, such as lime juice and chillies. It features in Middle Eastern, Asian, South American, Mexican and Mediterranean dishes.

4 dill

Dill's caraway-seed taste enhances egg, cucumber, potato, beetroot or fish. It can sometimes be mistaken for fennel leaves (which also have an aniseed flavour).

5 lemon grass

The tough outer leaves of this slender, tall herb are stripped away and the bases of the lemon-scented and lemon-flavoured internal stems are used. Lemon grass features in Thai and South-east Asian salads, especially those containing meat or fish.

6 marjoram

Traditionally used in Mediterranean and Mexican cooking, marjoram is a good complement to darker green salad leaves or tomato salads as well as warm salads containing courgettes and aubergine. It has a strong, spicy flavour. Use it sparingly. Marjoram is closely related to and similar in taste to oregano.

7 mint

This refreshing herb enlivens many kinds of salads and dessert fruit salads. You can steep the leaves in olive oil or white wine vinegar to make flavoured vinaigrettes. There are many varieties and their different flavours and aromas range from spearmint to apple and lemon.

8 parsley

Parsley is available all year. It comes in curly-leaved and flat-leaved (Italian) varieties. They are interchangeable, although flat-leaved is generally thought to have the finer flavour. Parsley is ideal in potato, mushroom or grain-based salads, among many others, and is often used simply as a garnish. Parsley is said to stimulate the appetite and to be good for rheumatism.

9 rocket

Another Mediterranean native that is used interchangeably as a salad green and herb, rocket has a peppery taste that becomes more pungent with age. Older leaves also tend to be coarser in texture. It can be used instead of basil in pesto.

Rosemary...it is sacred to remembrance and to friendship...

Sir Thomas More, writer, statesman and philosopher (1478–1535)

10 rosemary

The long, narrow leaves or needles of rosemary have an intense, slightly resinous, earthy taste. Popular in Mediterranean cooking, rosemary teams well with a number of other herbs including thyme, marjoram and parsley in herb vinaigrettes, oils and marinades. When very finely chopped, it can also be used in mushroom salads or salads that include meat or poultry.

11 tarragon

Tarragon, one of the classic French *fines herbes*, is used extensively in French cuisine. Its aniseed flavour works well in green salads as well as carrot, seafood, chicken or egg salads. Tarragon is also used to flavour vinegars, oils and mustards.

12 thyme

It is impossible to imagine the cooking of Provence and Italy without this herb. With its robust, spicy flavour, thyme complements a mix of salad greens as well as carrot, potato, mushroom, bean or pasta salads. A key ingredient, with parsley and bay, in a bouquet garni, it is also used to flavour oils and vinegars for marinades, vinaigrettes and dressings. Lemon thyme is another common variety. Lesser known, but also suitable for culinary use, are orange thyme and caraway thyme.

13 watercress

Rich in vitamin C, watercress has a hot, peppery taste. Sprigs can be used as a garnish or the leaves used in a variety of salads. Watercress is, in fact, a member of the high-nutrition cruciferous vegetable family to which broccoli and brussels sprouts belong.

Salad greens at a glance

A large variety of lettuce types and salad greens are now available to buy all year round, with new varieties appearing regularly. Visit your local farmers' market to look for new ones that your supermarket or greengrocer may not yet stock. Butterhead lettuces are soft and loose-hearted, while icebergs are dense and crunchy; cos lettuces have crisp, upright leaves. Loose-leaf lettuces don't form hearts; instead they are harvested as dense heads and, with no central core, the individual leaves are easily separated.

shopping

Freshness is the key to buying salad greens. Packaged, pre-washed salad green mixtures can be a useful, quick option at times, but putting together your own combination of leaves is by far the more flavoursome and creative way to go.

✳ Regardless of variety, lettuces, herbs and other salad greens should look clean and fresh with no wilted or slimy leaves.
✳ Avoid any produce that has yellowing leaves or rust-coloured or dark spots.
✳ Avoid lettuces that have a lot of tough outer leaves that will have to be discarded.

washing

All lettuces and salad greens need to be washed, even if they are labelled 'organic'. Packaged salad mixes should also be rinsed and the 'use-by' date noted. One of the best ways to wash and dry salad greens is to separate the leaves and then wash them in a sink full of cold water. Any very muddy or gritty leaves can be washed individually under cold, running water. Drain the leaves, shaking off excess water, and place them in a salad spinner and spin dry. If the leaves still seem a little wet, pat them dry with kitchen paper.

storing

The delicate varieties such as butterhead, oak leaf and lamb's lettuce, in particular, wilt within a couple of days of harvesting and lose their vitamin content. Crisper varieties such as iceberg lettuce, frisée lettuce, chicory and radicchio are more robust and will last longer.

✳ Salad greens are best kept in a cool, dark place, preferably in a sealed plastic container or in the vegetable crisper in the refrigerator.
✳ Do not add dressings or vinaigrettes until close to serving time because the acid that they contain will make the leaves wilt.

salads for health

Salads provide an easy, delicious way to enjoy a wide variety of foods and a host of essential nutrients. All kinds of fruits and vegetables can be included in a salad and, because these ingredients are mostly used raw, or are only briefly cooked, they retain the maximum amount of vitamins and minerals. For example, the vitamin C content of raw vegetables and fruit is higher than that of cooked. An added benefit is that raw foods take longer to chew and also take more time for the system to digest, so helping to curb the urge to overeat. Starchy carbohydrates, such as rice, potatoes, pasta, grains and bread, are important in a healthy diet and are easy to incorporate into salads. By adding moderate amounts of protein-rich food, such as meat, chicken, fish, nuts or eggs, a salad can be turned into a well-balanced and filling main dish. If weight-watching is an issue, it's important to be mindful of the choice and amount of dressing used. There are many low-fat options that taste just as good as their more calorific equivalents.

baby spinach

Glossy green spinach leaves have a slight metallic taste because of their iron content. The iron is not all absorbed by the body, due to the leaf's oxalic acid content. Spinach does contain many other valuable nutrients, especially antioxidants and bioflavonoids that may help block cancer-causing substances and processes. Use raw baby spinach leaves in salads for the best flavour.

Dressing A simple olive oil and vinegar dressing containing a few drops of walnut oil.

butterhead lettuce

Green and red butterhead lettuces are among the most popular varieties. They form small heads with soft, tender leaves. The heart is tender and the leaves have a mild flavour. Do not cut the large, floppy outside leaves; just tear them into bite-size pieces.

Dressing A light herb vinaigrette or a yogurt or sour cream dressing.

chicory

Also known as Belgian endive, this is a bullet-shaped head of smooth, compact, white to pale yellow leaves. The pale tones are the result of the plant not being exposed to sunlight during its growth. Crisp and succulent, witlof leaves have a bitter taste that works well in egg salads or in those that contain citrus fruits or celery.

Dressing A garlicky or herb dressing.

cos lettuce

This long, oval head of fairly tightly packed leaves has sturdy, rich green outer leaves and crisp white ribs. It has a mild, tangy flavour. Cos lettuce contains carotenoids and is rich in potassium.

Dressing A vinaigrette containing finely chopped hard-boiled eggs or crumbled feta cheese.

cress & sprouts

Salad cress (top) is a mixture of seedlings of garden cress and white mustard (or sometimes rape). It is commonly grown and used in the UK. The very delicate shoots taste peppery. They, like alfalfa or mung bean sprouts (bottom), are often used as a garnish, and also add plenty of texture to salads.

Dressing A classic vinaigrette with a few drops of hazelnut or sesame oil.

frisée

This is also known as curly endive. The large, slightly flattened round head has thin, light green leaves with wavy edges tapering to fine points. They have a bitter taste. The paler, greenish-yellow leaves at the centre form a compact heart. They are milder and more tender than the outer ones.

Dressing Thousand Island dressing and cream or sour cream dressings.

iceberg lettuce

A large, round, tightly packed lettuce that looks like a type of cabbage, iceberg has pale green leaves with a bland but refreshing taste. This lettuce is useful more for its crunch than its taste.
Dressing The mild taste works with all types.

lamb's lettuce

Also known as mâche, corn salad or field salad, this lettuce is comprised of small rosettes of pretty, delicate, mid-green leaves. They have a velvety texture and a mild flavour. Young leaves are the sweetest. Lamb's lettuce is high in beta carotene, which is thought to help fight heart disease and certain types of cancers.
Dressing Classic vinaigrettes using fruit vinegars, such as raspberry vinegar, and a few drops of walnut oil combined with olive oil.

lollo rossa & lollo bionda

These two Italian relatives of the butterhead lettuce form compact leaf rosettes without a firm head. They look very frilly because the ends of the reddish dark copper or light green leaves are finely crinkled, with lacy edges.
The crisp aromatic leaves are more robust than those of butter lettuce and will last a little longer.
Dressing A vinaigrette made with good-quality olive oil and balsamic vinegar.

mignonette

A loose-head lettuce, the mignonette has small, soft, mild-tasting leaves with ruffled edges. It is available in red and green varieties which look attractive mixed together in a salad. Because it is a loose-head lettuce with no firm core, the leaves are easy to pick individually.
Dressing Cream dressing with herbs.

nasturtiums

This plant with its bright orange, red and yellow blossoms looks attractive in mixed green salads and fruit salads. Other small, pretty flowers, such as pansies, violets or daisies or the flowers of edible herbs such as borage can be used. Be sure to wash flowers carefully and avoid any that have been sprayed with herbicides. Flowers vary greatly in taste from peppery to virtually tasteless and are valued more for their appearance than for their flavour.
Dressing All types of dressings.

oak leaf lettuce

The leaf shape gives this lettuce its name. Oak leaf is a loose-head lettuce with thin, tender reddish-brown or green scalloped leaves. They have a mild nutty flavour that teams well with mushroom or meat salads.
Dressing Stronger vinaigrettes with red wine vinegar or speciality vinegars such as cassis vinegar.

pak choi

This leafy, dark green vegetable is a Chinese variety of cabbage, which it resembles in taste. For salads, add raw chopped leaves and stems cut into thin strips.
Dressing An Asian-style dressing, including hot and spicy ingredients such as chillies and soy sauce, as well as crushed garlic and finely chopped fresh ginger.

radicchio

A member of the endive (chicory) family, radicchio is a tight head of crisp leaves that are a vibrant red or reddish-purple with white veins. It has a bitter, nutty taste that teams particularly well with citrus fruits. Treviso is a variety of radicchio with long, elongated leaves and a slightly milder flavour. Radicchio is high in beta carotene and other cancer-fighting phytochemicals.
Dressing A robust dressing, such as one containing mustard or blue cheese.

rocket

Also known as arugula, rocket is made up of clumps of rounded and spiked tender leaves that jut out from slender stems. Their distinctive peppery taste becomes more pronounced as the plant ages. Rocket goes well with tomatoes, feta, Parmesan, olives and roasted, marinated vegetables.
Dressing A vinaigrette made with balsamic vinegar and a little lemon juice.

sorrel

The elongated dark green leaves resemble spinach but are more oval or spear-shaped with a sharp, lemony taste. Slice leaves into thin strips and use sparingly with milder salad greens or other wild herbs or the taste can be overpowering. Use in white fish or salmon salads.
Dressing A mild dressing made with cream cheese or a more robust blue cheese.

You don't have to cook fancy or complicated masterpieces...just good food from fresh ingredients.

Julia Child, American cookbook author (1912–2004)

Oils

Oil, be it a fruity olive oil, an aromatic sesame or walnut oil or a mild safflower, peanut or rapeseed oil, gives a salad recipe its characteristic aroma and flavour. It also complements or accentuates the taste of the individual ingredients. For the best results and flavour, always buy the best oil that you can afford. Store oils in tightly sealed bottles in a dark, cool place, but not in the refrigerator. Nut oils have an intense flavour and should be used sparingly. They are more susceptible to spoilage and quickly turn rancid in hot conditions, so buy them in small quantities and use them as quickly as possible.

grapeseed oil

This oil varies in taste from delicately dry to mild and fruity. It is rich in the antioxidant vitamin E.

groundnut oil

The mild flavour is good for lighter salad dressings. It is a very good cooking oil for stir-frying as it does not intrude on the other flavours.

olive oil

Olive oil is the classic choice for most vinaigrettes. Different varieties of olive and varying growing regions and conditions will give the oil its own special properties, and it can be peppery, salty, fruity, creamy or mild. Ideally, have at least one basic mild extra virgin olive oil in your cupboard and experiment with other types. Olive oil, used in moderation, is considered to be one of the healthiest vegetable oils available, because it is high in monounsaturated fatty acids, which seem to help to lower blood cholesterol. Olive oil is also rich in phytochemicals and vitamin E.

rapeseed oil

A mildly nutty monounsaturated oil that is good in salads and for use as a general cooking oil.

safflower oil

One of the very mild, virtually flavourless oils, like sunflower, groundnut or rapeseed oil.

sesame oil

This is pressed from unroasted or roasted sesame seeds and ranges from mild to strong and darkly coloured. Use just a few drops combined with a more neutral-tasting oil. Use the darker type in oriental-style salads with chillies and soy sauce.

walnut and hazelnut oils

Only a few drops are needed, as with sesame oil. Use with another mild oil such as groundnut to impart just a hint of their flavour. The nutty tastes and aromas go well with salads that include cheese, chicken, celery, spinach, apples and green beans.

Vinegars

Vinegar has been used for many centuries to flavour and preserve food. Cider and wine are the common basic ingredients, but almost any product that can produce alcoholic fermentation can be used to make vinegar, as evidenced by the range used in this book, each with it's own particular qualities, including relative mildness and sharpness. You can create your own customised varieties by adding all kinds of fresh herbs, as well as chillies or fruit to cider or wine vinegars. Store in tightly sealed bottles in a dark place. The acid will keep the herbs or fruit from spoiling.

balsamic vinegar

Dark and richly complex in flavour, balsamic vinegar has a mild sweetness and a slight acidity that means that it can often be used on its own without oil. It originated in Modena, Italy, and is considered by many to be the best quality of vinegar available. It is produced from a type of red wine and the most prized, and expensive, varieties are aged from 15 to 50 years in wood barrels. Prices vary accordingly. Buy the best you can afford. Balsamic vinegar goes well with tomato or berry salads.

cider vinegar

Sharp and refreshing, this golden-coloured vinegar is good in dressings for cheese and ham salads.

To make a good salad is to be a brilliant diplomatist; the problem is entirely the same...to know exactly how much oil one must put with one's vinegar.

Oscar Wilde, Irish poet, novelist, dramatist and critic (1854–1900)

champagne vinegar

A mild, light vinegar fermented from champagne. Rice vinegar can be used in its place (see below). Champagne vinegar goes well in vinaigrettes and dressings for chicken, veal, fish or vegetable salads.

red wine & white wine vinegar

The classics, with red the slightly more robust, the taste depends on the wines used and their maturity. Sherry vinegar has an even fuller flavour. It goes with rice, grain, meat or fish salads. Cassis vinegar is a specialty vinegar made from blackcurrants and red wine. The bitter fruity vinegar goes well with oak leaf lettuce as well as mushrooms, beef or tuna.

rice vinegar

Used in Oriental cooking, spicy, aromatic rice vinegars are sweeter and milder than Western types because of a lower acid content. Use with rice or grain salads.

Herb dressings

Herb dressings look particularly appealing and go with many types of salads, such as green or vegetable salads, as well as with pasta or rice, fish or meat salads. To maximise the flavour, it's a good idea to make herb dressings in advance and store them in the refrigerator for a day or two. Then taste, and add more chopped fresh herbs just before serving. Make your own herb vinegars or oils and the results will be even better.

Raspberry nut herb vinaigrette

A good partner for bitter radicchio or peppery rocket leaves.

2 teaspoons hazelnut oil

3 tablespoons rapeseed or groundnut oil

2 tablespoons raspberry or other fruit vinegar

1 tablespoon Dijon mustard

salt and ground white pepper

2 spring onions, finely chopped

4 sprigs each parsley, tarragon, basil and dill

Whisk the two oils with the vinegar, mustard, salt and pepper. Add spring onions and finely chopped leaves of all the herbs. Note: Vary the types and amounts of herbs to suit different salad ingredients.

Raspberry vinegar

✳ Crush **500g fresh or frozen raspberries**. Add **500ml white wine vinegar**. Leave overnight.

✳ Press through a sieve into a sterilised jar. Add **375g caster sugar**; stir until the sugar has completely dissolved. Refrigerate or store in a cool, dark place for up to 2 weeks.

Classic herb vinaigrette

Good with all green salads and vegetable salads as well as grain or rice salads.

3 tablespoons white wine, sherry,
   or herb vinegar, or lemon juice
1 teaspoon Dijon or herb mustard
salt or herb salt and ground white pepper
4 tablespoons good-quality olive oil
5 small sprigs each parsley and dill
small bunch of chives
2 sprigs each marjoram and basil
pinch of sugar

Whisk vinegar, mustard, salt and white pepper in a bowl until salt has dissolved. Add olive oil, whisking until vinaigrette is slightly creamy. Chop herb leaves finely and stir into vinaigrette. Add sugar and more salt and pepper, to taste.

Lemon thyme vinaigrette

Use with green and vegetable salads, chicken, beef or seafood salads.

4 tablespoons olive oil
2 tablespoons lemon juice
1 teaspoon Dijon mustard
4 lemon segments, peel and pith removed
salt and ground white pepper
pinch of sugar
½ teaspoon lemon rind, grated
½ teaspoon fresh lemon thyme leaves, chopped

Combine olive oil, lemon juice and mustard in a bowl. Beat vigorously with a whisk. Chop lemon segments coarsely; whisk into vinaigrette. Season with salt, white pepper and sugar. Stir in lemon peel and lemon thyme.

Creamy sauce classics

Mayonnaise-style sauces that form a coating over salad ingredients are suitable for potato or pasta salads. Thin them with a little yoghurt or milk for more delicate green or vegetable salads. Some of these sauces are based on an egg yolk and oil combination. The eggs should be very fresh. (If you do not want to use raw eggs, buy good-quality mayonnaise in a jar.) The oil can be a neutral-tasting one such as sunflower or groundnut oil or a full-bodied olive oil. For the best result, use ingredients at room temperature.

Roquefort dressing

This tangy dressing goes well with mixed bean, green or vegetable salads.

50g Roquefort or Gorgonzola cheese

125g crème fraîche or light soured cream

2 tablespoons white wine vinegar

3 tablespoons fresh orange juice

1 tablespoon walnut oil

salt and freshly ground black pepper, to taste

generous pinch of sugar

3 tablespoons coarsely chopped walnuts, optional

Mash cheese finely with a fork in a bowl. Add crème fraîche and stir to make a smooth, creamy mixture. Add vinegar, orange juice and walnut oil and mix well. Add salt, pepper and sugar, to taste. Stir in chopped walnuts, if using.

Garlic sauce (aïoli)

The strong flavour is great with potato, meat, salmon or white fish salads.

1 large slice white bread, crust removed

2 to 3 tablespoons milk

3 cloves garlic, roughly chopped

1 teaspoon salt

2 medium very fresh egg yolks

250ml olive oil

1 tablespoon lemon juice

freshly ground black pepper

4 tablespoons yoghurt, optional

Tear bread into small pieces; drizzle with milk. Mix to a fine paste with garlic and salt. Using an electric whisk, add egg yolks and 2 tablespoons oil. Whisk in lemon juice, then another 2 tablespoons oil, drop by drop. Add remaining oil in a thin, steady stream; stir constantly. Add salt and pepper. Add yoghurt, if using.

Classic mayonnaise

Perfect for potato salads. Spices or herbs can be added to the recipe.

2 medium very fresh egg yolks
1 teaspoon Dijon mustard
2 tablespoons white wine vinegar or lemon juice
250ml olive oil
salt and freshly ground white pepper

Whisk egg yolks, mustard and vinegar in a medium bowl. Using an electric whisk, add oil, first drop by drop, then in a slow, steady stream. (If mixture curdles or splits, add a little hot water and beat vigorously.) Add salt and white pepper to taste. Refrigerate 1 to 2 days.

Thousand island dressing

Particularly good with fish and seafood salads, this is a very easy, quick recipe.

1 cup good-quality mayonnaise
125ml chilli sauce or tomato ketchup
few drops Tabasco (optional)
2 tablespoons pimiento-stuffed olives, chopped
2 tablespoons green pepper, finely chopped
1 tablespoon white onion, finely chopped
1 teaspoon pimiento, finely chopped
salt and freshly ground black pepper

Combine the ingredients and refrigerate. Add salt and pepper to taste, just before serving.

The Classics

Salads are an favourite dish all over the world and these globetrotting recipes take you from the USA to Russia, from the Middle East to Asia and from Europe to Africa. Many of the recipes included here have stood the test of time, truly earning their position as 'classics' in the repertoires of restaurant chefs and home cooks alike.

Caesar salad

In 1924 in Tijuana, Mexico, Caesar Cardini first mixed cos lettuce, Parmesan and croutons, dressed with garlic, lemon, egg, olive oil and Worcestershire sauce.

2 small heads cos lettuce

4 large leaves iceberg lettuce

50g Parmesan, in a piece

2 slices sourdough bread, crusts removed

2 tablespoons olive oil

anchovy dressing

4 anchovy fillets

1 clove garlic, roughly chopped

5 tablespoons olive oil

1 very fresh large egg yolk

2 tablespoons lemon juice

2 tablespoons Dijon mustard

1 tablespoon Worcestershire sauce

pinch of sugar

salt and freshly ground black pepper

serves 4

preparation 30 minutes

per serving 312 calories, 26g fat, 6g saturated fat, 12g carbohydrate, 3g sugar, 0.5g fibre, 1.4g salt

1 Cut cos and iceberg lettuce leaves into bite-size pieces. Use a vegetable peeler or cheese grater to shave Parmesan into thin slivers.

2 To make anchovy dressing, place anchovy fillets and garlic in a bowl and mash to a paste. Whisk in olive oil, egg yolk, lemon juice, mustard, Worcestershire sauce and sugar. Add salt and freshly ground black pepper, to taste.

3 To make croutons, cut bread into small cubes. Heat olive oil in a large nonstick pan over medium heat. Add bread cubes; cook until golden brown on all sides, taking care they do not burn. Set aside; keep warm.

4 Arrange lettuce leaves and shaved Parmesan on individual serving plates. Drizzle dressing over salad and sprinkle on bread cubes.

mix and match

＊ Omit olive oil and egg yolk from the anchovy dressing. Use **250g good-quality mayonnaise** instead.

＊ Add **2 cooked skinless chicken breasts (about 300g in total)** cut into strips to the salad.

Waldorf salad

Oscar Tschirky, maître d'hôtel of the Waldorf-Astoria Hotel in New York, first combined crunchy apples and celery with mayonnaise in 1896.

500g celery or celeriac

2 medium tart apples (about 300g)

3 tablespoons lemon juice

150g red grapes

100g walnuts

125g mayonnaise

pinch of sugar

salt and freshly ground black pepper

mint sprigs, for garnish

serves 4

preparation 25 minutes

----

per serving 448 calories, 41g fat, 5.5g saturated fat, 15g carbohydrate, 14g sugar, 4g fibre, 0.6g salt

1 Cut celery into fine matchsticks. Halve and core apples and cut or grate into fine strips. Place celery and apples in a bowl; stir in 2 tablespoons lemon juice to prevent discolouration.

2 Reserve a few grapes for garnish; halve and de-seed the rest. Reserve a few walnuts for garnish; coarsely chop the rest. Add halved grapes and chopped walnuts to bowl.

3 To make dressing, whisk mayonnaise with remaining 1 tablespoon lemon juice in a small bowl. Add sugar and salt and pepper to taste.

4 Stir dressing into salad. Garnish with reserved grapes and walnuts and top with mint sprigs.

Chef's salad

The Ritz-Carlton Hotel's 1940s version called for ox tongue as well as chicken and ham; earlier recipes used fruit and other vegetables with meat and lettuce.

2 skinless chicken breast fillets
  (about 300g in total)
oil, for brushing
1 large head cos lettuce
4 plum tomatoes, cut into wedges
150g thinly sliced ham
125g thinly sliced Emmental cheese
3 medium eggs, hard-boiled, thinly sliced

white wine vinaigrette

3 tablespoons olive oil
2 tablespoons white wine vinegar
1 teaspoon Dijon mustard
½ teaspoon sugar
salt and freshly ground black pepper

serves 4
preparation 10 minutes
cooking 15 minutes

per serving 427 calories, 28g fat, 10g saturated fat,
4.5g carbohydrate, 4g sugar, 1g fibre, 2g salt

1 Heat grill to medium-hot. Brush chicken with oil; cook about 5 minutes each side or until cooked through. Let stand 5 minutes; slice thinly.

2 Tear lettuce leaves into small pieces. Arrange on a large platter. Top with chicken, tomatoes, ham, cheese and eggs.

3 To make vinaigrette, whisk oil, vinegar, mustard and sugar until combined. Drizzle salad with vinaigrette and season with black pepper.

a bite of history

This salad is a flexible way to use ingredients that you may already have in your storecupboard or fridge: it can include various combinations of cold meats, cheeses, eggs and salad greens.

a bite of history

This salad was created in 1926 by Bob Cobb at the Brown Derby in Los Angeles. The story is that he wanted a snack and put together leftovers from the restaurant kitchen.

Cobb salad

A substantial and flavoursome salad of chicken, bacon, eggs, lettuce, tomatoes, avocado and blue cheese that is a protein-packed meal in itself.

500ml chicken stock

125ml dry white wine

1 small lemon, chopped

4 skinless chicken breast fillets
    (about 600g in total)

4 rashers bacon, chopped

3 medium eggs, hard–boiled, chopped

1 small head butterhead lettuce

2 cups trimmed watercress

3 medium tomatoes (about 500g, chopped)

1 large avocado, diced

150g blue cheese, crumbled

vinaigrette

3 tablespoons olive oil

2 tablespoons white wine vinegar

2 teaspoons finely chopped tarragon

1 teaspoon Dijon mustard

1 teaspoon honey

1 clove garlic, crushed

salt and freshly ground black pepper

serves 6

preparation 20 minutes

cooking 15 minutes

per serving 421 calories, 27g fat, 10g saturated fat, 5g carbohydrate, 4g sugar, 2.4g fibre, 1.6g salt

1 Combine stock, wine and lemon in a medium saucepan; bring to a boil. Reduce heat; add chicken. Simmer, covered, about 15 minutes or until cooked through. Drain chicken; cut into bite-size pieces. Leave to cool.

2 Cook bacon in a frying pan over high heat until crisp. Drain on kitchen paper.

3 Tear lettuce leaves into small pieces. Arrange lettuce and watercress on individual serving plates and top with chicken, bacon, eggs, tomatoes, avocado and cheese.

4 To make vinaigrette, whisk oil, vinegar, tarragon, mustard, honey and garlic until combined. Add salt and pepper to taste. Drizzle salad with vinaigrette.

cook's tip

Butterhead lettuces have soft, floppy leaves. To add crunch to this salad, use cos or iceberg lettuce.

Spinach, roasted garlic and parmesan

Thin shavings of Parmesan complement baby spinach, sun-dried tomatoes and whole cloves of roasted garlic, drizzled with a light balsamic dressing.

8 small cloves garlic, unpeeled

3 tablespoons olive oil

50g Parmesan, in a piece

300g baby spinach leaves

3 tablespoons pine nuts, roasted

90g drained sun-dried tomatoes

2 tablespoons balsamic vinegar

salt and freshly ground black pepper

serves 4

preparation 5 minutes

cooking 20 minutes

per serving 342 calories, 32g fat, 6g saturated fat, 5g carbohydrate, 4g sugar, 2g fibre, 1g salt

1 Heat oven to 180°C/gas 4. Place garlic in a small roasting pan; drizzle with 1 tablespoon of the oil. Roast about 20 minutes or until soft. Peel garlic.

2 Using a vegetable peeler, slice Parmesan into large, thin shavings.

3 Place garlic and Parmesan in a serving bowl with remaining ingredients. Add salt and pepper to taste. Toss gently to combine.

Stuffed avocado salad

Juicy prawns, mixed with watercress and spring onions
and a creamy dill dressing, make a lively filling for
fresh, buttery avocados.

2 spring onions

1 large lemon

1 tablespoon olive oil

1 tablespoon sherry vinegar

salt and freshly ground black pepper

175g cooked, peeled prawns

4 medium ripe avocados

50g trimmed watercress

dill dressing

125g soured cream

2 tablespoons crème fraîche (optional)

3 tablespoons finely chopped fresh dill

salt and freshly ground black pepper

serves 4

preparation 20 minutes

per serving 441 calories, 42g fat, 12g saturated fat,
5g carbohydrate, 2g sugar, 5g fibre, 0.8g salt

1 Finely dice spring onions. Cut lemon in half. Cut one
half into thin slices and squeeze juice from other half.

2 Whisk oil and vinegar until combined; add salt and
pepper to taste. Add spring onions and prawns. Marinate
while making dressing.

3 To make dill dressing, whisk soured cream, crème fraîche
(if using) and 1 teaspoon lemon juice in a bowl until creamy.
Add salt and pepper to taste. Stir in dill.

4 Cut avocados in half and remove stones. Remove flesh,
leaving a rim about 5mm wide. Dice flesh finely and mix
with 1 tablespoon lemon juice and a little salt.

5 Combine avocado, watercress, prawns and spring onions
and spoon into avocado shells. Spoon dill dressing on the
top. Garnish with lemon slices.

Three bean salad Tuscan-style

Cannellini beans, red kidney beans and fresh green beans, along with tomato and fresh onions are the basis for this classic Tuscan salad.

300g green beans, trimmed, halved

1 can (400g) red kidney beans,
   rinsed and drained

1 can (400g) cannellini or lima beans,
   rinsed and drained

1 small red onion, finely chopped

2 large tomatoes (about 350g),
   seeded, chopped

3 tablespoons chopped fresh
   flat-leaved parsley

3 tablespoons olive oil

2 tablespoons lemon juice

1 clove garlic, crushed

salt and freshly ground black pepper

serves 4

preparation 10 minutes

cooking 7 minutes

per serving 282 calories, 10g fat, 1.5g saturated fat, 36g carbohydrate, 8g sugar, 12g fibre, 0.9g salt

1 Half fill a medium saucepan with water and bring to a boil. Add green beans; cook 5 to 7 minutes or until just tender. Drain; rinse with cold water.

2 Combine green beans, kidney beans, cannellini beans, onion, tomatoes and parsley in a serving bowl. Mix oil, lemon juice and garlic. Add salt and pepper to taste. Stir into salad.

red kidney beans

A good source of fibre, protein, vitamin B_6 and vitamin C and containing many important minerals, these beans have a full flavour that complements fresh green beans.

mix and match

* Add **1 small green** or **red pepper**, finely diced. Add a generous pinch of **sugar** to the **oil**, **lemon juice** and **garlic** and season with **salt** and **pepper** to taste. Toss to combine.

* Use **400g borlotti beans**, rinsed and drained, in place of fresh green beans. Add **3 tablespoons chopped fresh coriander**.

American potato salad

Warm salad potatoes, crumbled hard-boiled egg and spring and red onions and mayonnaise are the basis for this much loved American classic, served slightly warm.

1kg waxy potatoes, peeled,
    cut into small pieces

2 tablespoons cider vinegar

3 medium eggs, hard–boiled, chopped

1 medium red onion, chopped finely

2 celery stalks, chopped finely

50g chopped dill pickles

4 tablespoons chopped fresh parsley

250g good–quality mayonnaise

2 teaspoons Dijon mustard

½ teaspoon celery seeds

salt and freshly ground black pepper

3 spring onions, sliced thinly

serves 6

preparation 15 minutes

cooking 12 minutes

per serving 468 calories, 35g fat, 6g saturated fat, 31g carbohydrate, 3g sugar, 2.5g fibre, 0.7g salt

why warm?

Potatoes are used warm in these two salads because they will absorb the flavours of the dressings. Dressings added to cold potatoes tend to 'sit' on them rather than soak in.

1 Half fill a large saucepan with water; add potatoes and bring to a boil. Reduce heat to a simmer, cook 10 to 12 minutes or until just tender. Drain.

2 Place warm potatoes in a large serving bowl; add vinegar and toss to combine. Add eggs, red onion, celery, pickles and parsley; toss gently.

3 Combine mayonnaise, mustard and celery seeds in a small bowl. Add salt and pepper to taste. Stir gently into salad. Top with spring onions.

Bacon and potato salad

Warm potatoes and hard-boiled eggs get a tangy boost from pickled cucumber and crispy bacon, dressed with mayonnaise and soured cream spiced with paprika.

1kg small new potatoes

5 rashers bacon, chopped

4 medium eggs, hard-boiled, quartered

50g chopped pickled cucumbers

3 tablespoons chopped fresh
flat-leaved parsley

150g good-quality mayonnaise

4 tablespoons soured cream

1 tablespoon lemon juice

1 teaspoon ground sweet paprika

2 tablespoons chopped fresh dill

serves 4

preparation 10 minutes

cooking 15 minutes

per serving 468 calories, 35g fat, 6g saturated fat, 31g carbohydrate, 3g sugar, 2.5g fibre, 0.7g salt

1 Half fill a large saucepan with water; add potatoes and bring to a boil. Reduce heat to a simmer, cook 10 to 12 minutes or until just tender. Drain and cut in half.

2 Cook bacon in a lightly oiled frying pan over high heat until crisp. Drain on kitchen paper.

3 Place warm potatoes in a large serving bowl; add eggs, cucumbers and parsley; toss gently.

4 Combine mayonnaise, soured cream, lemon juice and paprika in a small bowl. Add to salad and toss gently. Sprinkle bacon and dill on top.

cook's tip

Both the bacon and eggs can be cooked ahead of time and used cold in the finished salad. It is only the potatoes that must be used warm.

Coleslaw

From the Dutch *koolsla*, coleslaw is a salad of shredded cabbage mixed with mayonnaise. It is the archetypical picnic and barbecue salad and goes well with most cold, cooked meats.

½ head medium green cabbage (about 500g)

1 large carrot, grated

½ small onion, finely chopped

3 spring onions, thinly sliced

2 celery stalks, thinly sliced

3 tablespoons chopped fresh
   flat-leaved parsley

125g good-quality mayonnaise

2 teaspoons lemon juice

1 teaspoon Dijon mustard

salt and freshly ground black pepper

serves 4

preparation 10 minutes

----

per serving 270 calories, 25g fat, 4g saturated fat,
9g carbohydrate, 8g sugar, 5g fibre, 0.6g salt

1 Finely shred the cabbage using a sharp knife or a mandoline slicer (see page 11).

2 Place cabbage in a large bowl with carrot, onion, spring onions, celery and parsley; toss to combine. Whisk mayonnaise, lemon juice and mustard in a small bowl until well combined. Add salt and pepper to taste. Add dressing to salad; toss gently to combine.

mix and match

❋ **Mixed cabbage coleslaw** Replace half the green cabbage with **red cabbage** and add **1 tablespoon toasted caraway seeds**.

❋ **Fruity coleslaw** Add **1 large green apple** cut into matchsticks and **3 tablespoons sultanas** to basic coleslaw salad.

❋ **Crunchy nut coleslaw** Replace onion with **6 red radishes** cut into matchsticks; add **4 tablespoons toasted slivered almonds**.

Cucumbers with dill and soured cream dressing

In this German-style salad, a light but tasty dressing of soured cream with wine vinegar, Dijon mustard and fresh dill complements raw red onion and mild cool cucumbers.

2 large cucumbers (about 550g)

1 teaspoon salt

1 small red onion, thinly sliced

3 tablespoons chopped fresh dill

soured cream dressing

125g soured cream

2 tablespoons white wine vinegar

1 teaspoon sugar

2 teaspoons Dijon mustard

salt and freshly ground black pepper

serves 4

preparation + chilling 50 minutes

----

per serving 94 calories, 7g fat, 4g saturated fat, 6g carbohydrate, 5g sugar, 1g fibre, 1.2g salt

1 Cut cucumbers in half lengthways and scoop out seeds with a small spoon. Slice flesh thinly. Place cucumbers in a colander and sprinkle with salt. Let stand 15 minutes.

2 Rinse under cold water to remove excess salt; drain. Place cucumbers, onion and dill in a large bowl. Cover and refrigerate at least 30 minutes.

3 To make soured cream dressing, whisk soured cream, vinegar, sugar and mustard until combined. Add salt and pepper to taste. Spoon over cucumbers, onion and dill; toss gently to coat.

Tzatziki

✳ Peel **4 large cucumbers (about 1kg in total)**. Remove seeds and chop flesh finely. Place cucumbers in a colander; sprinkle with **2 teaspoons coarse salt**. Let stand for 15 minutes. Rinse under cold water to remove excess salt; drain.

✳ Place **500g Greek-style yoghurt** in a serving bowl; add the cucumber and **1 clove garlic, crushed**. Season with **salt** and **freshly ground black pepper**. Serve well chilled as a dressing or as a side salad.

Cucumbers with dill and soured cream dressing

Tex Mex salad

Pico de gallo, the Spanish term for rooster's beak,
is a fresh salsa made from chopped tomatoes,
onion and chillies (usually jalapeños or serranos)

2 skinless chicken breast fillets
(about 400g in total)
1 tablespoon vegetable oil
3 tablespoons enchilada sauce from a jar
4 large maize tortillas
1 large head cos lettuce
400g can red kidney beans,
rinsed and drained
1 large avocado, diced
2 tablespoons pickled hot chillies, chopped
2 sprigs flat-leaved parsley, for garnish

pico de gallo

2 large tomatoes (about 350g),
de-seeded, chopped
1 small red onion, finely chopped
1 fresh small red chilli, finely chopped
3 tablespoons fresh coriander, chopped
3 tablespoons vegetable oil
2 tablespoons lime juice
1 clove garlic, crushed

serves 4
preparation 20 minutes
cooking 15 minutes

per serving 503 calories, 26g fat, 4g saturated fat,
21g carbohydrate, 8g sugar, 8g fibre, 1.8g salt

1 Heat grill to medium hot.

2 Brush chicken with half the oil; cook 5 minutes each side or until cooked through. Leave 5 minutes; slice thinly.

3 Bring enchilada sauce to a boil in a medium saucepan; add chicken and toss to coat. Remove from heat and cover to keep warm.

4 Brush tortillas with remaining oil; cook under grill about 2 minutes each side or until browned lightly and crisp. Break into large pieces.

5 To make pico de gallo, combine tomatoes, onion, chilli and coriander in a small bowl; add combined oil, lime juice and garlic and toss to mix.

6 Chop or tear lettuce leaves into small pieces. Arrange lettuce on a large serving platter. Top with beans, avocado, jalapeños and pico de gallo. Arrange chicken on top and sprinkle with tortilla pieces. Garnish with parsley.

cook's tip

Replace chicken with a homemade chilli sauce, using the
same quantity of red kidney beans used in this recipe.
Substite tortilla chips for fresh maize tortillas.
Top with soured cream.

Salad with Camembert

Small, tasty leaves such as rocket, dandelion and frisée are the base for lightly fried Camembert, partnered by cranberries and a raspberry and cranberry vinaigrette.

100g rocket

50g dandelion leaves or extra rocket

½ head frisée lettuce

1 small wheel Camembert (about 125g)

1 medium egg

salt and freshly ground black pepper

100g dried breadcrumbs

2 tablespoons sunflower oil

50g fresh cranberries or precooked frozen cranberries

vinaigrette

2 tablespoons sunflower oil

2 tablespoons raspberry vinegar

2 teaspoons dried cranberries

1 shallot, finely diced

salt and freshly ground black pepper

serves 4

preparation 15 minutes

cooking 10 minutes

---

per serving 270 calories, 15g fat, 6g saturated fat, 21g carbohydrate, 2g sugar, 1.5g fibre, 1g salt

1 Place rocket, dandelion and lettuce in a serving bowl, tearing any large leaves into small pieces.

2 Cut Camembert into quarters. In a shallow bowl, beat egg with salt and pepper. Place breadcrumbs on a plate.

3 To make vinaigrette, whisk oil, raspberry vinegar, dried cranberries and shallot until combined; add salt and pepper to taste. Drizzle over salad.

4 Heat 2 tablespoons oil in a nonstick pan. Coat cheese in egg, then in breadcrumbs. In a frying pan, cook cheese over high heat, turning once, until golden brown. Drain on kitchen paper. Add cheese and cranberries to salad.

cook's tip

To cook frozen cranberries, cover with water; add a little sugar. Bring to a boil. Simmer just until they pop or they will become mushy. Add a little butter to stop the pan from boiling over.

Salad Niçoise

This Mediterranean salad is instantly redolent of its Provençale origins, with tuna, anchovies, egg, peppers and olives nestled amid crispy leaves.

150g fresh or frozen green beans

1 medium orange pepper

2 potatoes, boiled the previous day
   and left unpeeled

1 medium head cos lettuce

1 large tomato, cut into wedges

185g can tuna, in oil or water, drained

1 medium red onion, thinly sliced

4 medium eggs, hard–boiled, quartered

50g black olives

vinaigrette

4 tablespoons olive oil

3 tablespoons red wine vinegar

1 clove garlic, crushed

salt and freshly ground black pepper

serves 4

preparation 15 minutes

cooking 5 minutes

per serving 400 calories, 24g fat, 4.5g saturated fat, 24g carbohydrate, 6g sugar, 3.5g fibre, 1g salt

1 Cook beans in lightly salted water about 5 minutes or until crisp-tender. Drain and leave to cool. Cut into pieces.

2 Halve pepper and cut into strips. Peel potatoes; slice thinly. Tear lettuce leaves into strips. Mix beans, peppers, potatoes, lettuce and tomato in a large bowl.

3 To make vinaigrette, whisk oil, vinegar and garlic until combined; add salt and pepper to taste. Pour over salad.

4 Break tuna into pieces with a fork. Place tuna, onion, eggs and olives on salad

a bite of history

Salad niçoise is one of many classic salads that are open to interpretation. Usually the olives, potatoes, green beans and a vinaigrette dressing are regarded as essential. Some believe that the salad should be served on a bed of lettuce; others favour tomatoes as the base. Some cooks simply toss all the ingredients together.

Mozzarella, basil and tomatoes

Bite-size balls of fresh mozzarella are known as 'bocconcini', which is the Italian for 'mouthful'. The cheese is milky-white with a mild taste; olives and sharp cherry tomatoes add extra flavour.

300g drained baby mozzarella balls, cut in half

500g cherry tomatoes, cut in half

80g black olives

2 tablespoons fresh flat–leaved parsley, chopped

12 fresh basil leaves

2 teaspoons olive oil

salt and freshly ground black pepper

serves 4

preparation 15 minutes

per serving 260 calories, 20g fat, 11g saturated fat, 4g carbohydrate, 3.5g sugar, 1.5g fibre, 1.3g salt

1 Place mozzarella, tomatoes and olives in a serving bowl.

2 Sprinkle on parsley and basil. Drizzle salad with olive oil and add salt and pepper to taste. Toss gently to combine.

a bite of history

The green, white and red ingredients in this salad reflect its Italian origins and represent the colours of the Italian flag. The combination of mild mozzarella, aromatic basil and full-flavoured ripe tomatoes is a summer classic.

Tuscan white bean salad with tuna

Small white beans are at the heart of a number of Tuscan recipes. Here they're paired with a little tuna and flavoured with red onion, lemon juice and sage.

2 cans (400g) each white beans, drained and rinsed

1 can (425g) tuna, in oil or water, drained

1 medium red onion, sliced

3 tablespoons olive oil

3 teaspoons lemon juice

a few fresh sage leaves

1 tablespoon fresh parsley, chopped

serves 6

preparation 5 minutes

----

per serving 290 calories, 12g fat, 2g saturated fat, 18g carbohydrate, 2g sugar, 6.5g fibre, 0.5g salt

1 Toss beans, tuna, onion, oil, lemon juice and sage leaves together in a large serving bowl.

2 Sprinkle with chopped parsley just before serving.

cook's tip

Cannellini beans are traditionally used in this recipe, but any type of small white bean can be used as an alternative. Sage is popular in Italian cooking and is a good complement to cheese.

Italian bread salad

Bread salads are an excellent way to use bread that's slightly past its best. Moisten, then allow the absorbent bread to take on a host of flavours including tomatoes, celery and basil.

300g day–old ciabatta

1 large red onion, diced

2 medium tomatoes, diced

2 stalks celery, diced

2 small cucumbers, diced

3 sprigs oregano

4 tablespoons finely chopped fresh basil leaves

4 tablespoons olive oil

salt and coarsely ground black pepper

3 tablespoons good–quality red wine vinegar

serves 4

preparation + chilling 1 hour 10 minutes

per serving 331 calories, 14g fat, 2g saturated fat, 44g carbohydrate, 6g sugar, 3g fibre, 1g salt

1 Cut bread into large pieces and moisten with a little water. Soak briefly, squeeze to remove liquid, then tear into small pieces. Mix bread, onion, tomatoes, celery and cucumbers in a serving bowl.

2 Finely chop oregano leaves. Mix with basil, oil, salt and pepper. Pour over bread and vegetables. Chill, covered, about 1 hour. Stir in red wine vinegar. Season to taste.

ciabatta

Ciabatta, an oval, flattish yeast bread with an open texture and crisp crust, is ideal for this salad. Many frugal peasant dishes use day-old crusty bread as an ingredient.

Bread salad with roasted peppers

Toasty, crusty bread is mixed with the sweetness of roasted peppers and the delicious sharpness of feta and olives, then simply dressed with olive oil.

4 large red peppers, cut in half

1 tablespoon olive oil

300g crusty Italian or French bread, cubed

1 large tomato, diced

1 medium cucumber, diced

100g feta cheese, crumbled

80g black olives

serves 4

preparation 2 hours + 15 minutes

cooking 10 minutes

per serving 370 calories, 13g fat, 5g saturated fat, 54g carbohydrate, 12g sugar, 5g fibre, 2.6g salt

1 Grill peppers (see page 111). Peel skin; cut flesh into thin strips. Drizzle with oil. (Allow 2 hours.)

2 Heat oven to 190°C / gas 5. Spread bread cubes on a baking tray and bake, tossing occasionally, 5 minutes or until lightly crisped but not browned.

3 Combine peppers, toasted bread, tomato, cucumber, feta and olives in a large bowl, tossing well to combine. Serve at room temperature or chilled.

health guide

All cheeses contain casein, which is a substance that protects teeth naturally. The calcium and phosphorus in cheese helps remineralise tooth enamel.

Russian salad

In Russia, beetroot is on just about every menu. To preserve their vibrant colour and important nutrients, do not peel or cut them before cooking: just scrub gently.

500g fresh beetroot, trimmed

500g potatoes, peeled, cut into wedges

60g frozen peas

3 tablespoons sliced dill pickles

1 small red onion, finely sliced

3 tablespoons good–quality mayonnaise

3 tablespoons soured cream

2 teaspoons white wine vinegar

1 teaspoon Dijon mustard

serves 4

preparation 15 minutes

cooking 30 to 35 minutes

per serving 260 calories, 13g fat, 3g saturated fat, 35g carbohydrate, 11g sugar, 5g fibre, 0.6g salt

1 Half fill a large saucepan with water; add beetroot and bring to a boil. Cook 20 to 25 minutes or until just tender. Drain and cool. Peel; cut into wedges.

2 Half fill a medium saucepan with water; add potatoes and bring to a boil. Cook 8 minutes; add peas. Cook another 2 minutes or until vegetables are tender. Drain.

3 Combine beetroot, potatoes and peas in a large bowl; add pickles and onion. Whisk mayonnaise, soured cream, vinegar and mustard in a small bowl until smooth. Add to salad; toss gently to combine.

cook's tip

Ideally, cook beetroot a day ahead of when you need it. Chill, covered, until ready to use. If fresh beetroot is unavailable, use canned whole baby beetroot, drained.

mix and match

* Poach or pan-fry **2 skinless chicken breast fillets (about 300g in total)**. Cut into strips and add to salad.

* Thinly slice **300g cold roast duck or other game bird** and add to salad.

Herring and dill salad with potatoes

The key to this Scandinavian-inspired salad is the dressing of cream, yoghurt, horseradish and herbs – a perfect partner for pickled herring and new potatoes.

250g pickled herring in oil, drained

2 medium white onions

2 large dill pickles

4 potatoes, cooked the previous day
    and left unpeeled

herb cream

125g yoghurt

100g double cream

1 teaspoon grated horseradish paste

1 to 2 teaspoons lemon juice

3 tablespoons finely chopped
    fresh chervil

4 tablespoons finely chopped fresh dill

3 tablespoons finely chopped
    fresh flat–leaved parsley

salt and ground white pepper

serves 4

preparation + chilling 2 hours 25 minutes

per serving 415 calories, 18g fat, 7g saturated fat, 48g carbohydrate, 13g sugar, 3g fibre, 1.9g salt

1 Pat herring fillets dry and cut into small pieces. Thinly slice onions and cucumbers. Peel potatoes and slice.

2 Arrange potatoes on a platter. Place herring pieces on top. Place one third of the onion rings and cucumber slices on top of herrings.

3 To make herb cream, combine yoghurt and cream. Stir in horseradish, lemon juice and all the herbs; season with salt and pepper. Spoon over salad.

4 Refrigerate, covered, at least 2 hours. Let salad reach room temperature before serving. Garnish with remaining onion rings and sliced cucumbers.

Herring salad with radish and rocket

✳ Peel **1 white radish** and cut into thin sticks. Halve **250g cherry tomatoes**. Peel **1 medium red onion** and cut into thin rings. Remove stalks from **125g rocket**. Cut **250g ready-to-eat herring fillets** into small pieces and arrange on top of salad ingredients.

✳ Whisk **3 tablespoons olive oil** with **2 tablespoons lemon juice**. Season with **salt** and **pepper** and drizzle over salad.

Herring and dill salad with potatoes

Middle-Eastern bread salad

Originating in the Lebanon where it is called *fattoush*, this salad mixes bread, tomatoes and cucumber with a dressing of lemon, garlic, mint, parsley and coriander.

1 cucumber, seeded and diced

3 medium tomatoes, seeded and diced
(cubes should be about the same size
as the cucumber)

6 spring onions, finely chopped

salt and freshly ground black pepper

1 small iceberg lettuce, roughly chopped

3 small rounds pita bread

2 tablespoons olive oil

dressing

4 tablespoons olive oil

grated peel and juice of 1 lemon

2 cloves garlic, crushed

2 tablespoons fresh flat–leaved parsley,
roughly chopped

2 tablespoons fresh mint leaves,
roughly chopped

2 tablespoons fresh coriander leaves,
roughly chopped

serves 6

preparation 20 minutes

cooking 5 minutes

per serving 200 calories, 12g fat, 2g saturated fat, 23g carbohydrate, 4g sugar, 2g fibre, 0.5g salt

1 Combine cucumber, tomatoes and spring onions in a colander and sprinkle with salt. Leave 10 minutes to drain. Place in a serving bowl with lettuce.

2 Roughly tear pita bread into small pieces. Heat oil in a frying pan. Fry bread over medium heat until golden brown. Drain on kitchen paper to remove excess oil.

3 To make dressing, whisk all ingredients together until combined. Drizzle over salad; toss well to coat. Season with salt and pepper. Top with pieces of fried pita bread.

cook's tip

Pita bread can be toasted instead of fried. Separate each round into layers. Spray each one lightly with oil. Place on a baking tray; toast in a preheated 180°C/gas 4 oven for about 8 minutes or until golden. Break into small pieces.

a bite of history

For a traditional Middle Eastern touch, sprinkle the salad with a teaspoon of sumac, a purplish-red ground spice with a slightly sour, lime taste.

Tabbouleh

This favourite Lebanese salad is a satisfying combination of textures and flavours. For added health benefits, you could use twice the amount of parsley in place of the lettuce strips.

180g instant bulgur wheat or couscous

2 medium tomatoes, finely diced

1½ cucumbers, finely diced

4 spring onions, sliced

125g finely fresh flat-leaved parsley, chopped

75g finely chopped fresh mint

4 tablespoons olive oil

6 tablespoons lemon juice

salt and freshly ground black pepper

cos lettuce leaves, for serving

1 heart cos lettuce, cut into strips

mint and coriander sprigs, for garnish

1 large tomato, cut into wedges, for garnish

serves 4

preparation + standing 45 minutes

per serving 290 calories, 12g fat, 2g saturated fat, 40g carbohydrate, 5g sugar, 2g fibre, trace salt

1 Place bulgur wheat in a pan with 500ml water. Bring to a boil. Remove from heat; leave 20 minutes to absorb liquid. Fluff with a fork.

2 Combine bulgur, tomatoes, cucumbers, spring onions, parsley and mint in a bowl. Whisk oil and 4 tablespoons lemon juice; add salt and pepper to taste. Pour over salad and toss to combine; leave 30 minutes.

3 Arrange lettuce leaves on a large platter. Season tabouleh to taste with salt and remaining 2 tablespoons lemon juice; fold in lettuce strips. Arrange on lettuce leaves. Garnish with herb sprigs and tomato wedges.

health guide

This is a nutritious salad, containing plenty of fibre. When consumed in portions that contain at least 30g of leaves, fresh parsley provides useful amounts of vitamin C, iron and calcium.

cook's tip

Instant or quick-cooking couscous will give a quicker result. It needs about 10 minutes standing time after boiling.

Asian chicken salad

Ginger, chillies and lemongrass – along with fish sauce and lime juice – give a South-east Asian touch to minced chicken and onion.

1 tablespoon peanut or sunflower oil

1 tablespoon grated fresh ginger root

1 stalk lemongrass, chopped

2 fresh red chillies, chopped

2 cloves garlic, chopped

500g chicken mince

3 tablespoons fresh lime juice

1 tablespoon Asian fish sauce

1 teaspoon soft brown sugar

1 medium red onion, thinly sliced

2 tablespoons fresh mint, shredded

60g coriander leaves

1 small head cos or ½ small head iceberg
    lettuce, leaves separated

serves 4

preparation 10 minutes

cooking 6 minutes

----

per serving 170 calories, 4g fat, 0.7g saturated fat, 2g carbohydrate, 2g sugar, 0g fibre, 0.9g salt

cook's tip

For a quick version of this salad, buy a cooked chicken. Remove the skin and bones, then finely chop the chicken breast meat or shred it with a fork.

1 Heat oil in a large nonstick frying pan over medium heat. Add ginger, lemon grass, chillies and garlic. Cook 1 minute, stirring. Add chicken and cook, stirring, 5 minutes or until chicken is cooked.

2 Remove from heat and allow to cool slightly. Combine lime juice, fish sauce and sugar; pour over chicken.

3 Add onion, mint and coriander, reserving a few leaves for garnish. Toss gently. Place salad in individual bowls, garnish with remaining coriander. Scoop portions of salad onto lettuce leaves to form parcels or cups for eating.

Greek salad

Feta, tomatoes and olives are the key ingredients in most versions of this popular salad although it has many variations. It can also include rice-stuffed vine leaves and anchovies or, as here, chillies.

3 medium tomatoes

1 cucumber

2 large red onions

2 medium green peppers

100g black olives

100g pickled mild or hot chillies

4 tablespoons olive oil

2 tablespoons red wine vinegar

salt and freshly ground black pepper

300g feta cheese

1 teaspoon dried oregano or 2 teaspoons fresh oregano leaves

serves 4

preparation 20 minutes

per serving 392 calories, 31g fat, 13g saturated fat, 14.5g carbohydrate, 12g sugar, 4g fibre, 3.5g salt

cook's tip

In Mediterranean cooking, oregano and marjoram are interchangeable. They both have a warm, slightly sharp taste with an underlying spiciness. Oregano often has a lemony taste.

1 Cut tomatoes into wedges. Cut cucumbers into thick slices. Slice onions, not too thinly. Cut peppers into strips.

2 Place all the vegetables in a bowl. Top with olives and pickled chillies. To make vinaigrette, whisk 3 tablespoons oil and all the vinegar until combined; add salt and pepper to taste. Drizzle over salad.

3 Cut feta into thick cubes or crumble coarsely; add to salad. Sprinkle oregano on top and drizzle with remaining 1 tablespoon oil.

Thai beef salad with peanuts

Flash-fry thin strips of beef, then add peanuts and spices, including coriander, ginger and garlic for a Far-Eastern-inspired main-course salad that's cooled with cucumber and fresh mint.

3cm piece fresh ginger root

4 sprigs coriander

500g beef fillet

4 tablespoons sunflower oil

3 tablespoons lime juice

2 tablespoons soy sauce

½ teaspoon ground ginger

50g unsalted peanuts

2 medium red onions, thinly sliced

salt

2 spring onions

1 fresh red chilli

¼–½ cucumber, thinly sliced, for garnish

few mint sprigs, for garnish

serves 4

preparation 20 minutes

cooking 10 minutes

per serving 370 calories, 25g fat, 6g saturated fat, 7g carbohydrate, 5g sugar, 2g fibre, 1.5g salt

1 Peel ginger and chop finely. Chop coriander leaves finely. Cut beef into very thin strips.

2 Heat oil in a wok or deep frying pan. Sear meat on all sides over high heat, stirring, until no more juice escapes. Place in a bowl. Mix lime juice, soy sauce, ground ginger and fresh ginger and add to meat, stirring to combine.

3 Wipe wok or pan with kitchen paper. Dry-roast peanuts lightly over medium heat; add to meat. Stir red onions and coriander into meat. Season with salt.

4 Slice pale green and white parts of spring onions on the diagonal. Cut chilli in half, remove seeds. Cut into fine strips.

5 Spoon salad onto individual plates. Sprinkle with spring onions and chilli strips. Garnish with cucumber slices and mint leaves.

Spicy beef salad with pepper and corn

❋ Cut **500g beef fillet** into strips and fry as described in main recipe. Place in a bowl and mix with **2 tablespoons lime juice**, **1 tablespoon red wine vinegar**, **1 teaspoon ground cumin** and **1 crushed garlic clove**.

❋ Finely slice **2 red onions**. Cut **2 red peppers** into strips. Dice **3 tomatoes**. Add **150g canned sweetcorn kernels**, onions, peppers and tomatoes to beef, mix in and season with salt and pepper.

❋ Halve **2 red chillies** and chop finely. Heat **2 tablespoons sunflower oil** in a wok until very hot and briefly sauté chillies, stirring. Spoon salad onto plates. Top with chillies and **2 tablespoons chopped fresh coriander**.

Thai beef salad with peanuts

Gado gado

Gado means 'mixed'. This traditional Indonesian speciality is a combination of raw and lightly cooked vegetables served with a spicy peanut sauce.

1 small head iceberg lettuce, leaves separated

2 large potatoes, boiled and sliced

200g green beans, sliced, blanched

80g bean sprouts, blanched

125g shredded Chinese cabbage, blanched

2 medium tomatoes, cut into wedges

1 medium red onion, sliced

3 spring onions, cut in short lengths

½ cucumber, thinly sliced

2 fresh red chillies, seeded and thinly sliced

4 medium hard–boiled eggs, sliced

125g fried tofu, cut into cubes

peanut sauce

125ml vegetable oil

200g raw unsalted peanuts

2 cloves garlic, chopped

4 spring onions, chopped

salt

½ teaspoon chilli powder

1 teaspoon soft brown sugar

1 teaspoon soy sauce

500ml water

juice of 1 lemon

serves 6

preparation 30 minutes

cooking 15 minutes

per serving 515 calories, 39g fat, 6g saturated fat, 24g carbohydrate, 8g sugar, 5g fibre, 0.7g salt

1 Arrange lettuce leaves on a large plate. Add all the remaining salad ingredients in small groups (for people to help themselves). Serve peanut sauce separately.

2 To make peanut sauce, heat oil in a wok or frying pan over high heat. Stir-fry peanuts until light golden brown, about 4 minutes. Remove with a slotted spoon and place on kitchen paper to cool. Pound or process peanuts until finely ground. Discard oil from pan, reserving 1 tablespoon.

3 Crush garlic and spring onions in a mortar and pestle with a little salt. Fry in reserved oil, about 1 minute. Add chilli powder, sugar, soy sauce and water. Bring to a boil; add ground peanuts. Simmer, stirring occasionally, until sauce is thick, about 10 minutes. Add lemon juice and more salt, if needed. Cool. (Sauce can be made ahead and stored in a jar in the refrigerator for up to 1 week.)

a bite of history

Gado gado ingredients vary from region to region. Other additions are spinach, mangetout or cauliflower. Firm vegetables can be served raw, blanched or steamed. Whatever method is used, they must remain crunchy. Serve the salad cold or at room temperature.

Salad Greens & Vegetable Salads

Different kinds of lettuces and vegetables are the basis of countless attractive and nutritious side dishes and main meal salads. Choose the freshest and best seasonal ingredients you can find for each dish and add complementary or contrasting flavours with a variety of dressings and vinaigrettes.

Green salad with creamy chive yoghurt

What could be a standard side salad is enlivened by croutons fried in basil butter and a soured cream and yoghurt dressing, laden with chives.

3 heads cos lettuce

2 spring onions, thinly sliced

vinaigrette

1 tablespoon olive oil

1 tablespoon white wine vinegar

1 tablespoon lemon juice

1 teaspoon Dijon mustard

salt and freshly ground black pepper

creamy chive yoghurt

170g light soured cream

3 tablespoons yoghurt

30g chopped chives

salt and freshly ground black pepper

croutons

3 thick slices of bread

2 tablespoons butter mashed with
    1 teaspoon fresh basil, finely chopped

serves 4

preparation 15 minutes

cooking 3 to 4 minutes

per serving 216 calories, 14g fat, 7g saturated fat, 19g carbohydrate, 5g sugar, 1g fibre, 0.7g salt

1 Chop lettuces into wide strips. Place in a serving bowl.

2 To make vinaigrette, whisk oil, vinegar, lemon juice and mustard until combined; add salt and pepper to taste. To make creamy chive yoghurt, combine soured cream, yoghurt and chives; add salt and pepper to taste.

3 To make croutons, cut bread into small cubes. Melt herb butter in nonstick pan over medium heat. Add bread cubes; cook until golden brown on all sides, taking care butter does not burn. Set aside; keep warm.

4 Drizzle vinaigrette over lettuce. Toss to coat. Sprinkle with spring onions. Spoon on dressing; top with croutons.

cook's tip

Herb butters for cooking croutons are easy to make. Mash a little finely chopped garlic or chives into the butter as an alternative, or another fresh seasonal herb.

Green salad with creamy herb yoghurt

* Combine a mixture of salad greens, such as **rocket, oak leaf and iceberg**, in a bowl. Make vinaigrette and croutons as for main recipe.

* To make creamy herb yoghurt, combine **2 tablespoons each chopped fresh dill, chives, tarragon, parsley** and **watercress** with **soured cream** and **yoghurt, salt** and **pepper**, as for main recipe. Drizzle vinaigrette over salad leaves; toss to coat. Spoon creamy herb yoghurt over the top. Add croutons.

Green salad with creamy chive yoghurt

Curly lettuce salad with eggs and crisp bacon

Dainty leaves of frisée lettuce are threaded through with thin strips of crispy bacon. The vinaigrette has a base of tarragon and is sharpened with mustard and horseradish.

1 large head frisée lettuce

5 spring onions, finely sliced

4 tablespoons vegetable oil

4 thin slices bacon, sliced lengthways

4 medium eggs

mustard horseradish vinaigrette

5 tablespoons tarragon or other
   herb vinegar

generous pinch of hot mustard powder

1 teaspoon horseradish sauce, or to taste

salt and freshly ground black pepper

serves 4

preparation 15 minutes

cooking 10 minutes

per serving 271 calories, 24g fat, 5g saturated fat, 2g carbohydrate, 2g sugar, 0.6g fibre, 1g salt

1 Tear or chop lettuce into small pieces. Divide among serving plates. Sprinkle evenly with spring onions.

2 To make vinaigrette, whisk 2 tablespoons of the oil, 2 tablespoons of the vinegar, mustard and horseradish until combined. Add salt and pepper to taste. Drizzle over salad ingredients.

3 Half fill a large saucepan with water. Add remaining 3 tablespoons vinegar; bring to a boil. Heat remaining 2 tablespoons oil in a frying pan. Add bacon; fry until crisp. Keep warm.

4 One at a time, break eggs onto a plate and slide them into the boiling water. Reduce heat to a simmer. Poach eggs 4 to 5 minutes, or until cooked as desired. Remove with a slotted spoon and drain. Trim ragged edges. (Alternatively, hard-boil the eggs; peel and slice when cooled.) Place 1 egg on each serving of salad. Top with bacon. Serve immediately.

Salad with egg vinaigrette

Finely diced eggs give plenty of texture to the white wine and herb vinaigrette that adds excitement to a simple salad of crisp lettuce, red onion and tomatoes.

1 large head cos or iceberg lettuce

4 medium tomatoes

1 small red onion, thinly sliced into rings

egg vinaigrette

2 medium eggs, hard-boiled

30g each fresh basil and fresh flat-leaf parsley, finely chopped

30g chives, chopped

2 leaves fresh lemon balm, chopped

2 sprigs marjoram, leaves finely chopped

3 tablespoons olive oil

1 tablespoon white wine vinegar

1 tablespoon lemon juice

pinch of sugar

salt and freshly ground black pepper

serves 4

preparation 20 minutes

- -

per serving 153 calories, 12g fat, 2g saturated fat, 6.5g carbohydrate, 6g sugar, 2g fibre, 0.2g salt

1 Tear or chop lettuce into small pieces. Divide among serving plates. Halve and core tomatoes; cut into eighths. Arrange around lettuce. Top with onion rings.

2 To make egg vinaigrette, peel eggs and dice very finely. Combine all the chopped herbs.

3 Whisk oil, vinegar and lemon juice in a medium bowl until combined. Stir in chopped eggs and herbs. Add sugar and salt and pepper to taste. Drizzle over salad ingredients.

Mushroom salad

Sweet shallots, earthy mushrooms and fragrant chopped herbs are sautéed briefly together with a little wine vinegar and port, then added to a bed of colourful leaves and dried cranberries.

1 head red or green oak leaf lettuce,
   or a mixture of both
250g brown cap or chanterelle mushrooms
2 sprigs rosemary
4 sprigs thyme
3 tablespoons olive oil
3 shallots, finely chopped
2 tablespoons red wine vinegar
2 tablespoons port wine
salt and freshly ground black pepper
2 tablespoons crème fraîche or
   light soured cream
3 tablespoons dried cranberries

serves 4
preparation 10 minutes
cooking 12 minutes

per serving 170 calories, 12g fat, 3.5g saturated fat,
3g carbohydrate, 3g sugar, 2g fibre, trace salt

1 Tear lettuce into small pieces. Use to line a serving bowl. Wipe mushrooms with kitchen paper. Trim and cut large ones in half. Finely chop rosemary and thyme leaves.

2 Heat oil in a large frying pan. Sauté shallots until transparent. Add mushrooms and cook until golden brown, stirring occasionally. Add chopped herbs, saving a little for garnish; sauté briefly.

3 Add vinegar and port wine to mushroom mixture. Cook, uncovered, until mixture is slightly reduced, about 2 minutes. Add salt and pepper to taste. Spoon over prepared salad. Spoon a little crème fraîche or light soured cream onto each portion. Sprinkle with dried cranberries.

Lettuce, carrot and fennel salad with vinaigrette

A bulb of fennel, complete with its feathery fronds, along with the more exotic taste of lemon balm, gives special flavour to a base of curly lettuce and radiccio.

4 tablespoons sunflower seeds

1 head red lettuce, such as oak leaf

1 small head radicchio

2 medium carrots (about 250g)

1 medium fennel bulb (about 500g), with leafy fronds

fresh lemon balm leaves, for garnish

lemon and sherry vinaigrette

2 tablespoons lemon–flavoured olive oil

1 tablespoon sherry vinegar

1 tablespoon lemon juice

3 tablespoons tomato juice

salt and freshly ground black pepper

serves **4**

preparation + cooking **25 minutes**

per serving 183 calories, 13g fat, 2g saturated fat, 11g carbohydrate, 8g sugar, 6g fibre, 0.2g salt

1 Toast sunflower seeds in a frying pan over medium heat until golden, stirring occasionally. Transfer to a plate; set aside to cool. Tear or chop lettuce and radicchio into small pieces; arrange on a serving platter.

2 Coarsely grate carrots. Cut fennel bulb into thin slices. Place carrots and fennel on top of lettuce. Finely chop a few fennel fronds; set aside.

3 To make lemon and sherry vinaigrette, whisk oil, vinegar, lemon juice and tomato juice until combined. Add salt and pepper to taste. Add to salad and toss. Add sunflower seeds, fennel fronds and lemon balm leaves.

cook's tip

Raw fennel can be difficult to digest. To avoid this problem, first cook the fennel bulb in lightly salted boiling water for 3 to 4 minutes. Cool in iced water.

Turkish carrot salad with garlic yoghurt

Cooked or raw carrots were first used in salads in north-western Africa. Lightly mixed with a yoghurt-based dressing and then chilled for about an hour, this salad is excellent served with warmed pita bread.

500g Greek-style yoghurt

3 tablespoons olive oil

4 medium carrots (about 500g), coarsely grated

2 cloves garlic, crushed

2 to 3 tablespoons lemon juice (or more, as liked)

salt and freshly ground black pepper

flat-leaved parsley sprigs, for garnish

serves 4

preparation + chilling 1 hour 30 minutes

cooking 10 minutes

----

per serving 284 calories, 22g fat, 10g saturated fat, 16g carbohydrate, 14g sugar, 3g fibre, 0.3g salt

1 Line a large sieve with coffee filter paper or muslin; place over a large bowl. Spoon yoghurt into sieve. Leave to strain for 20 minutes.

2 Heat oil in a nonstick pan over medium heat. Add carrots; cook, stirring occasionally, 10 minutes, or until almost soft. Remove from heat; leave to cool.

3 Combine strained yoghurt and carrots in a serving bowl. Add garlic and 2 tablespoons lemon juice; toss. Add more lemon juice, if needed, and salt and pepper to taste.

4 Cover salad and chill for at least 1 hour. Taste again just before serving, adding lemon juice, salt and pepper, as liked. Spoon into serving bowls; garnish with parsley.

Fresh beetroot salad with yoghurt

✳ Wash **500g fresh beetroot**. Boil in a saucepan with plenty of water for 1 to 1 hour 30 minutes until soft. Drain and rinse under cold water. (Take care; the juice stains clothing.)

✳ Prepare **yoghurt** as described in main recipe and combine with grated beetroots. Season as described. Add **1 tablespoon olive oil** just before serving. Serve garnished with **parsley sprigs**

Turkish carrot salad with garlic yoghurt

cook's tip

Low-fat yoghurt will stay runny after straining. Ideally, use a thick, Greek-style, full-fat yoghurt to achieve the correct, thick consistency.

Carrot salad

Not just a carrot salad, this dish is packed with hazelnuts, sultanas, parsley and shredded coconut, with an orange and cumin-flavoured dressing.

4 medium carrots (about 500g), peeled, cut into matchsticks

60g flat-leaved parsley leaves

4 tablespoons shredded coconut, toasted

3 tablespoons hazelnuts, toasted, chopped

3 tablespoons sultanas

3 tablespoons olive oil

2 tablespoons orange juice

1 teaspoon ground cumin, toasted

serves **4**

preparation **15 minutes**

----

per serving 277 calories, 12g fat, 6.5g saturated fat, 19g carbohydrate, 18g sugar, 5g fibre, trace salt

1 Place carrots, parsley, coconut, hazelnuts and sultanas in a medium serving bowl.

2 Combine oil, juice and cumin and stir into the salad. Divide salad among individual serving bowls.

cook's tip

Most nuts benefit from toasting before being used in a recipe. The process brings out the flavour and reduces any bitter taste. Toast nuts just before you need to use them.

Moroccan-style carrot salad

Also known as *chizu*, cooked carrots are minced and then stirred through with a sweet and spicy dressing that contains cumin, ginger and lemon and orange juices.

4 medium carrots (about 500g), thickly sliced

2 teaspoons vegetable oil

1 teaspoon ground coriander

1 teaspoon ground cumin

¼ teaspoon ground ginger

pinch of salt

2 teaspoons honey

2 tablespoons lemon juice

1 tablespoon orange juice

4 tablespoons finely chopped fresh coriander leaves

serves 4

preparation + standing 25 minutes

cooking 8 minutes

----

per serving 66 calories, 2g fat, 0.5g saturated fat, 12g carbohydrate, 11g sugar, 2g fibre, 0.6g salt

1 Cook carrots in boiling water for 5 minutes, or until slightly softened. Place in a food processor with a little of the cooking liquid; process just until roughly chopped. Transfer to a serving dish.

2 Heat oil in a nonstick frying pan over medium heat. Add ground coriander, cumin, ginger and salt. Cook 2 to 3 minutes, or until aromatic. Add spice mixture to carrots; toss to coat. Add honey; toss again.

3 Combine lemon juice, orange juice and chopped coriander. Pour over salad. Leave for 10 minutes to allow the flavours to develop.

Red and green salad with champagne vinaigrette

A luxurious salad for a special occasion, with hard-boiled eggs stuffed with caviar and a dressing made with champagne vinegar.

1 head red lettuce, such as lollo rossa

1 heart pale lettuce, such as butterhead

4 small eggs, hard-boiled

4 large radishes, thinly sliced

1 tablespoon mayonnaise

1 tablespoon red or black caviar (optional)

watercress sprigs, for garnish

champagne vinaigrette

3 tablespoons olive oil

2 tablespoons champagne vinegar

1 tablespoon Dijon mustard

pinch of sugar

salt and freshly ground black pepper

serves 4

preparation 20 minutes

- -

per serving 210 calories, 18g fat, 3.5g saturated fat, 2g carbohydrate, 2g sugar, 1g fibre, 0.8g salt

1 Tear or chop both lettuces into small pieces. Arrange on a serving platter. Peel eggs and cut in half.

2 To make champagne vinaigrette, whisk oil, vinegar and mustard until combined. Add sugar and salt and pepper to taste. Drizzle vinaigrette over salad greens. Add radishes. Toss to combine.

3 Place a little mayonnaise on each egg half. Top with caviar, if using. Place egg halves on top of salad greens. Garnish with watercress.

heirloom varieties

Check out your local farmers' market for unusual types of lettuces. Heirloom varieties feature leaves in shades of red, green or yellow. Try contrasting the various colours.

Mixed salad greens with avocado

Add extra goodness to a green salad with the rich taste and superfood benefits of avocado, then dress simply with lemon juice and olive oil.

1 tablespoon olive oil

1 tablespoon lemon juice

1 teaspoon Dijon mustard

pinch of salt

350g mixed salad greens, such as iceberg lettuce, radicchio and rocket

1 medium red onion, thinly sliced

1 large avocado, peeled and diced

serves 4

preparation 5 minutes

per serving 143 calories, 13g fat, 2.5g saturated fat, 4.5g carbohydrate, 3g sugar, 3g fibre, 0.6g salt

1 Whisk oil, lemon juice, mustard and salt in a serving bowl until combined.

2 Add salad greens and red onion. Toss well to coat with dressing. Add avocado; toss to combine.

health guide

Although creamy-tasting avocados are high in fat, it is mostly the monounsaturated variety. This type of fat helps to lower blood levels of low-density lipoprotein – the so-called bad cholesterol.

Mangetout and lettuce salad with crunchy croutons

Blanch mangetout for a minute, then put them together with leaves, spring onions and bean sprouts. Serve with garlic croutons.

500g mangetout

crisp hearts of 2 green lettuces

3 spring onions, finely sliced

2 tablespoons vegetable oil

2 tablespoons white wine vinegar

salt and freshly ground black pepper

trimmed bean sprouts or cress, to garnish

2 thick slices wholegrain bread

1 tablespoon butter

1 clove garlic, peeled, sliced lengthways

serves **4**

preparation **20 minutes**

cooking **5 minutes**

per serving 165 calories, 9g fat, 3g saturated fat, 15g carbohydrate, 5g sugar, 4g fibre, 0.4g salt

1 Blanch mangetout in lightly salted boiling water 1 minute. Immerse in iced water; drain. (See step–by–step instructions below.)

2 Tear lettuce into pieces. Distribute among serving bowls. Add mangetout; sprinkle with spring onions.

3 To make vinaigrette, whisk oil, vinegar and a generous seasoning of salt and pepper. Drizzle over salad greens. Sprinkle with bean sprouts.

4 To make croutons, cut bread into small cubes. Heat butter in a nonstick frying pan over medium heat. Add garlic, cut surfaces face down. Fry 30 seconds; remove from pan and discard. Place bread cubes in garlic butter; cook until golden brown on all sides, taking care butter does not burn. Serve salad topped with hot croutons.

to blanch mangetout

1 Mangetout require minimal cooking. Blanching is ideal for brief cooking and retains the fresh colour of the vegetable. Trim tips from mangetout and remove any strings.

2 Place trimmed mangetout in lightly salted boiling water. Cook over high heat 1 minute.

3 Remove from boiling water with a slotted spoon. Immerse in iced water to cool and retain their bright green colour. Drain.

Multi-layered salad with yoghurt mayonnaise

Layered salads are very versatile. You can vary the type of bean or try chicken instead of ham, or a firm blue cheese instead of gouda. Choose ingredients that will give an attractive mix of colour when viewed from the side.

180g canned sweetcorn, drained

275g canned white beans, drained

1 head iceberg lettuce

1 red and 1 yellow pepper

250g ham, in one piece

200g gouda, in one piece

20 medium radishes

4 medium sweet and sour dill pickles

2 slices pumpernickel bread (optional)

yoghurt mayonnaise

250g yoghurt

175g mayonnaise

2 tablespoons milk

½ teaspoon English mustard

2 tablespoons sunflower or olive oil

1 tablespoon white wine vinegar

1 tablespoon lemon juice

½ teaspoon ground sweet paprika

salt and freshly ground black pepper

80g fresh parsley, finely chopped

30g fresh dill, finely chopped

60g chives, finely chopped

leaves of 3 sprigs thyme, chopped

serves 6

preparation + chilling 1 hour 40 minutes

per serving 590 calories, 40g fat, 12g saturated fat, 32g carbohydrate, 12g sugar, 6g fibre, 2.9g salt

1 Rinse sweetcorn and beans. Chop lettuce into strips. Cut peppers in half, discard seeds and chop into dice.

2 Trim ham of excess fat. Dice finely. Cut cheese into narrow strips. Chop radishes into quarters. Chop cucumbers into rounds.

3 Layer salad ingredients in a tall glass serving bowl in the following order: lettuce, radishes, corn, ham, pickles, peppers, cheese, beans.

4 To make yoghurt mayonnaise, place yoghurt, mayonnaise and milk in a bowl. Whisk in mustard, oil, vinegar and lemon juice. Add sweet paprika and salt and pepper to taste. Be generous with the seasonings. Fold in herbs. Pour dressing over salad. Chill, covered, 1 hour. Crumble pumpernickel bread, if using, over salad just before serving.

health guide

Sunflower oil is an all-purpose cooking oil with a mild taste. It is low in saturated fat. Use mild-tasting peanut oil or a richer flavoured olive oil, if you prefer the taste; they are also healthy options.

Italian-style layered salad

✳ In a glass serving bowl, layer **4 plum tomatoes, chopped, 150g torn rocket leaves, 2 red peppers, seeded and chopped, 250g sliced mozzarella, 2 cos lettuce hearts, torn into small pieces, 120g black olives, 250g artichoke hearts, chopped,** and **1 small cucumber, diced.**

✳ Mix **3 tablespoons homemade or purchased pesto, 3 tablespoons olive oil, 2 tablespoons lemon juice** and **4 tablespoons chicken or vegetable stock.** Add **salt** and **pepper** to taste. Pour over salad. Chill, covered, 1 hour. Serve with **toasted ciabatta** or **sourdough bread.**

**Multi–layered salad
with yoghurt mayonnaise**

Marinated vegetable salad

You can vary this simple salad according to the vegetables that are at the peak of their growing season and flavour. Mix textures, flavours and cheerful colours to give an enticing visual display. Blanch broccoli and squash briefly if you prefer a slightly less crunchy texture.

100g sliced broccoli and/or cauliflower florets

150g cherry tomatoes, halved

1 large carrot, cut into matchsticks

2 small yellow squash or 1 small courgette, thinly sliced

30g celery, finely sliced

marinade

125ml balsamic vinegar

125ml olive oil

3 tablespoons fresh parsley, chopped or fresh coriander leaves

1 tablespoon sugar

2 tablespoons fresh dill, finely chopped or 2 teaspoons dried dill

½ teaspoon salt

¼ teaspoon freshly ground black pepper

serves 4

preparation 25 minutes

marinating 8 hours or overnight

per serving 300 calories, 24g fat, 3.5g saturated fat, 17g carbohydrate, 16g sugar, 2.5g fibre, 0.6g salt

1 Place vegetables in a large, heavy-duty plastic bag. To make marinade, place all ingredients in a screw-top jar and shake well to combine.

2 Pour marinade over vegetables and seal top of bag. Store in refrigerator 8 hours or overnight, turning the bag occasionally to ensure vegetables absorb the maximum flavours from the marinade.

3 Use a slotted spoon to transfer the vegetables to a serving bowl. Serve at room temperature.

cauliflower

We're all used to seeing cauliflowers with heads of creamy white curd. Now, lime green as well as purple and orange varieties are also available. Use a mixture in this recipe to create a very appealing salad.

Salad with celery and mint dressing

✳ Slice **6 large red radishes** into rounds and add to salad ingredients in main recipe. Replace celery with **1 small finely sliced cucumber**.

✳ For the marinade, add **1 tablespoon finely chopped celery leaves**. Use **finely chopped fresh mint** in place of dill and **celery salt** in place of salt. Celery salt and celery leaves accentuate the taste of tomatoes.

Marinated vegetable salad

cook's tip

Always store tomatoes at room temperature. Refrigeration spoils their taste and texture. Slightly underripe tomatoes will ripen quickly in a brown paper bag.

Russian salad with potato and capers

Lucien Olivier, the chef at Moscow's Hermitage restaurant, developed a version of Russian salad in the 1860s. His recipe included both meat and fish, while the modern interpretation tends to be based on egg, potato, capers and peas.

500g waxy potatoes

200g carrots

1 large red pepper

250ml vegetable stock

150g green beans, cut into 5cm lengths

120g frozen peas

2 medium eggs, hard-boiled

3 tablespoons chopped fresh parsley

mayonnaise

1 medium egg yolk

pinch of mustard powder

generous pinch of salt

freshly ground black pepper

125ml vegetable oil

1 to 2 tablespoons lemon juice

2 tablespoons small capers plus
    2 to 3 tablespoons brine from the jar

serves 4

preparation + chilling 1 hour 30 minutes

cooking 15 minutes

----

per serving 422 calories, 29g fat, 4g saturated fat, 32g carbohydrate, 9g sugar, 6g fibre, 2g salt

1 Peel potatoes and cut into small cubes. Cut carrots and pepper into small cubes.

2 Bring stock to a boil in a large saucepan. Add potatoes, carrots and beans. Cook, covered, over medium heat, 5 minutes. Add peppers and peas. Cook, covered, another 5 minutes. Transfer vegetables to a sieve; leave to cool.

3 To make mayonnaise, make sure all the ingredients and the bowl are at room temperature to prevent curdling. Whisk egg yolk, mustard powder and a generous pinch of salt until creamy. Add oil in a thin stream, whisking until mixture thickens. Add 1 tablespoon lemon juice and salt and pepper to taste. Add 2 tablespoons caper brine. Taste, adding more brine, if liked.

4 Place vegetables and capers in a serving bowl. Spoon on mayonnaise, stirring to coat. Place in refrigerator 1 hour.

5 Just before serving, add more salt, pepper and lemon juice to taste. Peel eggs; slice into wedges. Add to salad. Sprinkle with parsley.

cook's tip

It's worth making double the quantity of this salad because it keeps very well and the flavours intensify. Cover and store in the refrigerator for up to 3 days.

Russian salad with potato and capers

Potato salad with cucumber

❋ Cook **800g waxy potatoes** in boiling water until just cooked. Drain, rinse under cold water. Cool, peel and slice. Finely slice **1 small red onion** and **1 small cucumber, seeds removed**. Place in a serving bowl.

❋ To make vinaigrette, whisk **3 tablespoons white wine vinegar, 4 tablespoons olive oil, ½ teaspoon hot mustard** and **4 tablespoons vegetable stock** until combined. Add **salt and pepper** to taste. Mix with salad. Cover and refrigerate for 30 minutes.

❋ Just before serving, add salt, pepper, vinegar and stock to taste. Sprinkle with **chopped chives**.

Root vegetable salad with spicy vinaigrette

Beetroot tastes sweet because it is richer in natural sugar than any other vegetable. Small beetroot with their leaves still attached have the most flavour. They go beautifully with a range of salad dressings.

600g beetroot

500g waxy potatoes

3 medium tomatoes

2 spring onions, finely chopped

2 cloves garlic, finely chopped

40g fresh flat–leaved parsley, finely chopped

3 sprigs coriander leaves finely chopped

100g black olives, for garnish

spicy vinaigrette

5 tablespoons white wine vinegar

6 tablespoons olive oil

½ teaspoon salt

pinch of freshly ground black pepper

pinch of cayenne pepper

serves 4

preparation + chilling 1 hour

cooking 1 hour 30 minutes

----

per serving 350 calories, 21g fat, 3g saturated fat, 35g carbohydrate, 13g sugar, 6g fibre, 1.4g salt

1 Place beetroot in a large saucepan, cover with water and bring to a boil. Cook 1 hour 30 minutes, or until a fork is easily inserted. Drain, reserving 4 tablespoons cooking water. Refresh under cold running water; leave to cool.

2 Cook potatoes in boiling water 20 to 30 minutes, or until just cooked. Drain, refresh under cold running water; leave to cool. Peel beetroot and potatoes, halve and slice thinly. Place in separate bowls.

3 Plunge tomatoes into boiling water 1 minute. Transfer to bowl of iced water. Peel tomatoes, cut in halves, remove seeds and dice flesh. Combine tomatoes and spring onions with beetroot. Add garlic, parsley, coriander and reserved cooking water.

4 To make spicy vinaigrette, whisk vinegar, oil, salt, pepper and cayenne pepper until combined. Stir two thirds vinaigrette into beetroot mixture and remainder into potatoes. Cover and refrigerate 30 minutes.

5 Just before serving, add salt, pepper and more vinegar to taste. Spoon beetroot salad onto a platter and arrange potato salad around it. Garnish with olives.

Mixed salad with caperberries

Caperberries give a unique tang to this appealing mixed salad. If you can't find them you can use capers – the unopened flower buds of the caper bush – instead, but they are less strongly flavoured.

800g waxy potatoes

150g rocket, roughly chopped

2 medium red onions, finely sliced into rings

200g cherry tomatoes, halved

60g each green and black olives, pitted

caperberry vinaigrette

2 to 3 tablespoons sherry vinegar

50g caperberries or capers plus 1 to 2
   tablespoons brine from the jar

1 teaspoon Dijon mustard

4 tablespoons olive oil

salt and freshly ground black pepper

serves 4

preparation + chilling 40 minutes

cooking 20 minutes

per serving 330 calories, 17g fat, 2.5g saturated fat, 41g carbohydrate, 7g sugar, 5g fibre, 2g salt

1 Cook potatoes in boiling salted water for 20 minutes, or until just cooked. Rinse under cold running water. Peel and dice when cool enough to handle. Place potatoes, rocket, onions, tomatoes and olives in a serving bowl.

2 To make caperberry vinaigrette, whisk vinegar, 1 to 2 tablespoons caperberry brine, mustard and oil until combined. Add salt and pepper to taste. Pour vinaigrette over salad and toss gently to combine.

3 Leave salad, covered, in a cool place 30 minutes. Add more salt, pepper and vinegar to taste. Slice caperberries in half and add to salad.

cook's tip

If the potato salad becomes a little dry while standing, add 2 tablespoons or so of hot stock. Let stand 5 minutes before serving.

Light potato salad with baby spinach

✳ Cook and peel **800g potatoes** as described in the main recipe; cut into rounds instead of dice.

✳ Finely slice **3 spring onions**. Tear **150g baby spinach leaves** into small pieces. Place salad in a bowl. Whisk **125g low-fat yoghurt**, **125g light soured cream**, **1 tablespoon white wine vinegar**, **1 tablespoon lemon juice** and **2 tablespoons olive oil** until combined. Pour over and toss through salad. Add **salt** and **pepper** to taste.

Mixed salad with caperberries

caperberries

Caperberries are the fruit of the caper bush. They are about 2cm long and are pickled in brine with their stems intact. They are available from delicatessens and some supermarkets. You can eat them whole as part of an antipasto plate. Alternatively, they can be sliced for use as a garnish.

Artichoke and herb salad with white beans

Tender artichoke hearts, salty ham and buttery white beans are the core of this wonderful salad. Add slices of plum tomatoes, then scatter rocket leaves and a few sprigs of rosemary to garnish.

4 large globe artichoke hearts
   (in oil and vinegar, from a jar)
100g ham, in one piece
4 tablespoons olive oil
2 cloves garlic, finely chopped
4 tablespoons dry white wine
4 sprigs thyme, leaves finely chopped
2 sprigs marjoram, leaves finely chopped
1 sprig rosemary, leaves finely chopped
40g fresh flat-leaved parsley, finely chopped
250g canned white beans, drained and rinsed
2 plum tomatoes, sliced
150g rocket, torn into small pieces
salt and freshly ground black pepper
2 to 3 tablespoons lemon juice

serves 4
preparation 10 minutes
cooking 5 minutes

per serving 290 calories, 22g fat, 2g saturated fat, 12.5g carbohydrate, 3g sugar, 4g fibre, 0.8g salt

1 Cut artichoke hearts into even pieces. Cut ham into dice, discarding any excess fat.

2 Heat 2 tablespoons oil in a nonstick pan. Add garlic; cook, stirring, just until transparent. Add artichoke pieces and wine. Cook over high heat, covered, 2 minutes. Add ham and herbs; heat briefly. Set pan aside and let mixture cool to lukewarm. Transfer to a serving bowl.

3 Add beans, tomatoes and rocket to artichoke mixture. Add salt, pepper and remaining lemon juice and oil to taste.

globe artichokes

The globe artichoke is the large flower bud of a bushy thistle plant. Its edible portions are the buttery heart and the earthy-tasting fleshy part at the base of the outer leaves. Steaming, boiling or baking are the best cooking methods. To prepare for cooking, see page 112.

Bean salad with paprika vinaigrette

cook's tip

Flat-leaved or Italian parsley tends to have more flavour than curly parsley. Avoid using dried parsley in salads as it has little flavour and none of the true parsley taste.

Bean salad with paprika vinaigrette

If you remove the skins from broad beans, their flavour is enhanced. Paprika in the vinaigrette adds an eastern European touch – it's Hungary's favourite flavouring.

600g frozen or shelled fresh broad beans,
  with skins removed if liked

1 small cucumber

2 shallots, finely diced

3 plum tomatoes, sliced

1 small red and 1 yellow pepper,
  seeded and diced

40g fresh flat-leaved parsley, finely chopped

paprika vinaigrette

4 tablespoons olive oil

2 tablespoons balsamic vinegar

1 tablespoon lemon juice

1 teaspoon ground cumin

½ teaspoon ground sweet paprika

pinch of cayenne pepper

pinch of freshly ground black pepper

serves 4

preparation 15 minutes

cooking 15 minutes

per serving 240 calories, 13g fat, 2g saturated fat,
21g carbohydrate, 11g sugar, 12g fibre, trace salt

1 Place beans in a saucepan. Cover with lightly salted water; bring to a boil. Cook 15 minutes or until crisp-tender. Drain and leave to cool.

2 Cut cucumber in half lengthways and remove seeds with a teaspoon. Slice cucumber thinly. Combine broad beans, cucumber, shallots and tomatoes in a serving bowl.

3 To make paprika vinaigrette, whisk ingredients until combined. Stir in diced peppers.

4 Arrange salad on individual plates. Drizzle on vinaigrette. Sprinkle with parsley.

Bean salad with cream dressing

✳ Cook **broad beans** as described in main recipe and allow to cool. Peel and finely dice **2 shallots** and place in a bowl with the broad beans.

✳ To make dressing, whisk **2 tablespoons white wine vinegar, 1 tablespoon olive oil, 3 tablespoons whipping cream, 2 tablespoons crème fraîche** or **light soured cream** and **salt** and **freshly ground black pepper** to taste. Stir dressing into salad. Cover and refrigerate 30 minutes. Serve with **wholegrain bread**.

Mixed bean salad with spicy cream dressing

You can vary the kinds of beans in this salad according to availability but try to choose an attractive mix of colours for maximum effect.

250g green beans

250g butter or broad beans, either fresh or frozen

140g canned red kidney beans, drained and rinsed

200g cherry tomatoes, sliced

1 large red onion, finely sliced

80g fresh flat–leaved parsley, finely chopped

salt and freshly ground black pepper

spicy cream dressing

1 clove garlic, roughly chopped

¼ teaspoon salt

4 tablespoons crème fraîche or light soured cream

2 teaspoons tomato purée

1 tablespoon olive oil

2 tablespoons balsamic vinegar

freshly ground black pepper

pinch of sugar

1 to 2 pinches of cayenne pepper

serves 4

preparation 10 minutes

cooking 15 minutes

per serving 204 calories, 10g fat, 5g saturated fat, 22g carbohydrate, 9g sugar, 7g fibre, 1.1g salt

1 Chop green beans into short lengths. Place in a steamer basket over a pan of simmering water. Cover pan; steam beans for 12 to 15 minutes until crisp-tender. Cook butter or broad beans for 6 minutes, or until tender. Remove from pan; leave to cool.

2 To make spicy cream dressing, place garlic in a mortar with ¼ teaspoon salt; grind to a fine paste. Mix with remaining dressing ingredients.

3 Combine salad ingredients in a serving bowl, adding salt and pepper to taste. Serve dressing separately.

health guide

Steaming is one of the cooking methods that best preserves the nutritional value, taste and texture of vegetables. Water and stock are both suitable as steaming liquids.

**Mixed bean salad
with spicy cream dressing**

Bean salad with crisp bacon

✻ Prepare **1kg butter beans**, as for main recipe. Cook 5–6 minutes in lightly salted boiling water. Drain and let cool.

✻ Finely dice **2 shallots**. Place in a bowl with the beans.

✻ Combine **4 tablespoons olive oil**, **2 tablespoons tarragon vinegar**, **salt** and **pepper** and pour over bean mixture. Leave in a cool place 2 hours, then season to taste. Grill or pan-fry **4 slices bacon** until crisp. Chop and sprinkle over salad while still warm. Sprinkle with **chopped fresh parsley.**

Fennel and green bean salad

Many kinds of canned beans will work well in this recipe. Try a combination of small and large canned beans of different colours. The fennel and courgette with a hot-citrus dressing, add a sharper note to the mellow beans.

grated rind and juice of 1 small orange

1 teaspoon wholegrain mustard

1½ tablespoons olive oil

1 clove garlic, crushed

1 (400g) can flageolet or navy (haricot) beans, drained and rinsed

80g pitted green olives

salt and freshly ground black pepper

1 medium fennel bulb, about 500g, sliced

150g green beans, halved

2 courgettes, about 200g in total, sliced

6 slices Parma ham or other prosciutto, about 90g in total, fat removed and slices halved

serves **4**

preparation **10 minutes**

cooking **5 to 10 minutes**

- -

per serving 218 calories, 10g fat, 2g saturated fat, 18g carbohydrate, 5g sugar, 9.5g fibre, 0.7g salt

1 Combine orange rind and juice, mustard, olive oil, garlic, flageolet beans and olives in a shallow baking dish. Season with salt and pepper to taste.

2 Bring a pan of salted water to a boil. Add fennel and green beans; simmer 1 minute. Add courgettes; cook another 4 minutes or until vegetables are just tender. Meanwhile, preheat grill to high.

3 Drain vegetables and combine with mixture in baking dish. Scrunch up Parma ham slices and arrange on top. Place dish under grill 1 to 2 minutes, sufficient to warm ham.

health guide

Recipes that use fennel sometimes list celery as an alternative. Although they are similar in texture, the nutritional differences between the two are significant. Fennel provides more potassium, vitamin C and folate than celery and has much more fibre.

cook's tip

Parma ham is the best known and one of the most expensive of the Italian salted, air–dried prosciutto. Pancetta (salt–cured bacon) may also be used.

Aubergine salad with tahini

This Mediterranean dish – popular from Greece to North Africa – has a deliciously smoky and nutty taste and a creamy texture. Serve it with wedges of warm pita bread.

2 large aubergines (about 600g)

7 tablespoons lemon juice

3 tablespoons tahini (sesame seed paste) from a jar plus 1 tablespoon oil from jar

3 cloves garlic, crushed

salt

2 tablespoons pomegranate seeds, for garnish (optional)

fresh parsley, chopped, for garnish

serves 4

preparation + chilling 1 hour 20 minutes

cooking 25 to 30 minutes

per serving 120 calories, 10g fat, 1.5g saturated fat, 4.5g carbohydrate, 4g sugar, 4g fibre, trace salt

1 Heat oven to 240°C / gas 9. Line a baking tray with aluminium foil. Wash aubergines; place on foil while wet. Bake 25 to 30 minutes, turning occasionally.

2 Rinse cooked aubergines under cold running water. Cut in half, scoop flesh into a bowl and drizzle with 3 tablespoons lemon juice to prevent discolouration.

3 Mash aubergine flesh in a bowl. Mix in tahini and 1 tablespoon oil from the jar, 3 tablespoons lemon juice and the garlic. Cover and refrigerate at least 1 hour.

4 Just before serving, add remaining 1 tablespoon lemon juice and salt to taste. Garnish with pomegranate seeds, if using, and parsley.

cook's tip

Buy large aubergines to get the maximum amount of flesh. Store them in a cool place but not in the refrigerator because aubergines tend to soften and become bitter. Cook them within a couple of days of purchase.

Aubergine salad with chillies and cumin

✳ Cut **2 large aubergines** into large dice. Place in a bowl; stir in **2 teaspoons salt**. (Aubergines can be bitter; salting helps rid them of the taste.) Set aside for 20 minutes. Wash aubergines; pat dry with kitchen paper.

✳ Heat **6 tablespoons olive oil** in a pan. Add aubergines; fry until golden brown. Add more oil, if necessary. Remove from heat. Leave to cool. Place in a serving bowl.

✳ Place aubergines in a serving bowl. Slice **2 mild green chillies** into strips and add to bowl. Combine **3 tablespoons lemon juice**, **1 teaspoon ground cumin**, **salt** and **pepper**. Stir into salad. Serve with **pita bread** and **tomatoes**.

Aubergine salad with tahini

tahini

Tahini is a paste made from ground sesame seeds. It is a key ingredient in hummous and other Middle-Eastern recipes. Tahini is available from most supermarkets as well as delicatessens and health food stores and is sold both salted and unsalted. Once opened, it will keep in a sealed jar in the refrigerator for several weeks.

mixing mayonnaise

1 Place egg yolk, garlic paste and half the lemon juice in a mixing bowl. Whisk vigorously for about 1 minute.

2 Beat oil into mixture a drop at a time at first. The mixture will gradually thicken.

3 Whisk in remaining oil in a thin, steady stream until well combined. Add yoghurt and remaining lemon juice; whisk briefly. Season to taste.

Asparagus salad with lemon and garlic mayonnaise

Choose tender asparagus at the peak of the season for this special salad or side dish. Substitute Parma ham or prosciutto for the smoked ham.

1kg medium–thick asparagus spears

1 teaspoon sugar

generous pinch of salt

200g smoked ham, trimmed of excess fat

fresh parsley, for garnish

lemon and garlic mayonnaise

1 clove garlic, roughly chopped

½ teaspoon salt

1 medium egg yolk

1 tablespoon lemon juice

3 tablespoons olive oil

2 tablespoons lemon–flavoured olive oil

125g yoghurt

salt and ground white pepper

serves **4**

preparation **15 minutes**

cooking **20 minutes**

----

per serving 283 calories, 20g fat, 4g saturated fat, 9g carbohydrate, 8g sugar, 4g fibre, 2.2g salt

1 Remove woody ends from asparagus. Half fill a large saucepan with water, add sugar and salt and bring to a boil. Add asparagus, cook 7–8 minutes, depending on thickness, or until crisp-tender. Remove asparagus from pan. Drain; keep warm until serving.

2 Cut ham into wide strips and arrange over base of serving dish.

3 To make lemon and garlic mayonnaise, pound garlic and salt to a fine paste in a medium bowl. Add egg yolk and ½ tablespoon lemon juice. Whisk vigorously until thickened.

4 Whisk both olive oils into the mixture, drop by drop, until it starts to thicken. Add remainder in a thin, steady stream until well combined. Add yoghurt and remaining lemon juice. Season to taste with salt and white pepper.

5 Place asparagus on top of ham, coat with a little mayonnaise and sprinkle with parsley leaves. Serve remaining mayonnaise in a separate bowl.

Radish and cucumber salad

In this fresh and appealing summer accompaniment that's both pretty and tasty, the hot peppery flavour of white and red radishes is cooled by cucumber.

1 large white radish, peeled
salt
1 medium cucumber
16 medium red radishes, thinly sliced
40g fresh parsley, chopped
30g chives, chopped
mung bean sprouts, for garnish

vinaigrette
1 tablespoon white wine vinegar
1 tablespoon lemon juice
3 tablespoons peanut oil
salt and freshly ground black pepper

serves 4
preparation 25 minutes

----

per serving 90 calories, 8g fat, 1g saturated fat, 2g carbohydrate, 2g sugar, 0.5g fibre, trace salt

1 Using a vegetable peeler or sharp knife, cut white radish into very thin curls. Place in a colander, sprinkle with salt and leave to drain for 15 minutes. Rinse and pat dry with kitchen paper.

2 Peel away thin strips the length of the cucumber to create a striped effect. Slice cucumber very thinly; arrange on individual plates or a serving platter. Place red and white radishes on top of cucumber slices.

3 To make vinaigrette, whisk vinegar, lemon juice, oil and salt and pepper to taste in a bowl. Drizzle over radishes. Top with chives and mung bean sprouts.

Cucumber salad

A creamy mustardy dressing with dill and spring onions gives piquancy to wafer thin slices of cucumber and radish. Salt the cucumbers beforehand to reduce some of their moisture.

1 medium cucumber

¼ teaspoon salt

2 large spring onions with green stems, finely sliced

4 medium red radishes, thinly sliced

soured cream dressing

125g soured cream

2 tablespoons tarragon vinegar or white wine vinegar

1 tablespoon fresh dill, finely chopped or 1 teaspoon dried dill

1 teaspoon sugar

1 teaspoon Dijon mustard

¼ teaspoon freshly ground black pepper

serves 4

preparation 40 minutes

chilling 1 hour

per serving 81calories, 6.5g fat, 4g saturated fat, 4g carbohydrate, 4g sugar, 0.5g fibre, 0.6g salt

cook's tip

The process of salting cucumbers removes some of the liquid so that the flavour of a dressing is not heavily diluted. It also helps to remove any residual bitter taste that the cucumbers may have.

1 Slice cucumber in half lengthways and scoop out seeds with a teaspoon. Slice cucumber thinly. Place in a bowl, sprinkle with salt and let stand 30 minutes. Drain, pat dry. Place cucumber, spring onions and radishes in a large bowl.

2 To make soured cream dressing, whisk soured cream, vinegar, dill, sugar, mustard and pepper until combined. Spoon over cucumber mixture. Toss to coat. Cover and refrigerate 1 hour.

Egg and radish salad

Both of the salad greens – frisée lettuce and chicory – used in this recipe have a slightly bitter taste that goes well with the peppery heat of the radishes and a herby cream cheese dressing.

2 medium eggs, hard–boiled
8 large frisée lettuce leaves
2 medium heads chicory
2 spring onions
16 medium red radishes

cream cheese dressing

100g cream cheese with herbs
    or plain cream cheese
3 tablespoons yoghurt
2 tablespoons herb vinegar
2 tablespoons rapeseed oil
2 tablespoons finely chopped fresh herbs
    such as a mixture of parsley, chives,
    dill, chervil or sorrel
salt and freshly ground black pepper

serves **4**
preparation **25 minutes**

per serving 255 calories, 22g fat, 9g saturated fat, 3g carbohydrate, 2g sugar, 1g fibre, 0.4g salt

1 Slice eggs into thin rounds. Divide frisée among serving plates. Place chicory leaves on top, open sides upwards.

2 Finely chop white part of spring onions; slice green part into thin rounds. Finely dice radishes. Mix with white part of spring onions.

3 To make cream cheese dressing, combine cream cheese, yoghurt, vinegar and oil. Add herbs, reserving a little for garnish. Season with salt and pepper.

4 Sprinkle radish/spring onion mixture evenly over the chicory. Top with dressing. Add egg slices. Sprinkle with remaining herbs and green parts of spring onions.

health guide

Rapeseed oil (often marketed as canola oil) is one of the world's major oil crops. It is a neutral-tasting oil that is very low in saturated fat. You can use safflower or groundnut oil as alternatives.

Warm grilled mixed vegetable salad

Use a ridged griddle pan to get attractive char-grilled strips on the vegetables as they cook. Mix peppers, courgettes, red onions, baby aubergines and mushrooms, then top with olives and oregano and serve warm.

500g green peppers, seeded and thickly sliced

500g red peppers, seeded and thickly sliced

500g courgettes, thinly sliced lengthways

1 large red onion, cut into wedges

6 baby aubergines, thinly sliced lengthways

150g portobello or large field mushrooms, thickly sliced

3 tablespoons olive oil

1 medium head treviso or round radicchio

120g pitted black olives

2 tablespoons balsamic vinegar

1 tablespoon finely chopped fresh oregano

serves **4**

preparation **20 minutes**

cooking **15 minutes**

per serving 270 calories, 16g fat, 2.5g saturated fat, 27g carbohydrate, 23g sugar, 10g fibre, 0.8g salt

1 Heat grill until medium-hot.

2 Mix peppers, courgettes, onion, aubergines, mushrooms and 1 tablespoon oil in a large bowl. Cook vegetables on grill plate until browned and tender, turning occasionally to cook evenly.

3 Place warm vegetables in a serving bowl. Add treviso, olives, vinegar, oregano and remaining 2 tablespoons oil. Toss gently to combine.

health guide

Mushrooms contain very few calories and are virtually fat-free. To get the maximum nutrients, store mushrooms for no more than five days in the refrigerator.

cook's tip

Grill an extra quantity of vegetables. Cool; place in a glass container. Pour in olive oil to cover. Seal jar and store in a cool place away from direct light. Serve as part of an antipasto plate.

Grilled tomato salad

Grilling tomatoes intensifies their flavour, especially if you choose naturally sweet plum tomatoes. Use ripe but firm tomatoes that will keep their shape during cooking.

10 plum tomatoes, halved lengthways

2 cloves garlic, finely sliced

150g rocket

90g pitted green olives

croutons

4 thick slices baguette

3 tablespoons olive oil

vinaigrette

2 tablespoons olive oil

1 tablespoon balsamic vinegar

1 tablespoon lemon juice

salt and freshly ground black pepper

serves 4

preparation 10 minutes

cooking 10 minutes

per serving 313 calories, 19g fat, 3g saturated fat, 32g carbohydrate, 10g sugar, 4g fibre, 1.2g salt

1 Heat grill to medium-hot. To grill tomatoes, place cut-side up on a baking tray. Sprinkle with garlic. Place under grill 2 to 3 minutes. Turn and cook another 2 minutes.

2 To make croutons, slice bread into small cubes. Heat 3 tablespoons of the olive oil in a nonstick frying pan over medium heat. Add bread cubes; cook until crisp on all sides. Set aside.

3 Tear rocket into small pieces. Arrange on serving plates. To make vinaigrette, whisk balsamic vinegar, lemon juice, salt, pepper and remaining oil until combined.

4 Place grilled tomatoes on top of rocket. Drizzle with vinaigrette. Add olives and croutons.

tomatoes

Tomatoes are a wonder food. One medium tomato contains more than half the daily requirement for vitamin C. Tomatoes also contain a phytochemical called lycopene that protects against prostate cancer and is known to slow damage to human cells caused by ageing and disease.

Grilled tomato salad

Grilled tomato salad with cheese

❋ Thickly slice **600g large tomatoes** or use **cherry tomatoes** and cut in half. Grill as for the main recipe, but for 2 or 3 minutes only. Place in a serving bowl with **1 medium red onion** sliced into thin rings.

❋ To make vinaigrette, whisk **4 tablespoons olive oil, 2 tablespoons red wine vinegar, salt, freshly ground black pepper** and **2 tablespoons chopped fresh mixed herbs** until combined. Stir into salad.

❋ Cut **250g feta or baked ricotta** into cubes. Sprinkle over salad. Add **chopped fresh basil leaves**. Serve with **ciabatta**.

Summer pepper salad

Select peppers with firm, glossy skin that feel heavy for their
size. You can make a one-colour salad or use a variety of peppers.
Red, yellow or orange peppers taste sweeter than green.

1kg green, red, yellow and orange peppers,
cut in half lengthways

4 tablespoons olive oil

2 tablespoons red wine vinegar

salt and freshly ground black pepper

serves **4**

preparation + chilling **1 hour 15 minutes**

cooking **15 minutes**

....

per serving 181 calories, 12g fat, 2g saturated fat,
16g carbohydrate, 15g sugar, 4g fibre, trace salt

1 Heat grill until hot. Or, heat oven to 240°C/gas 9.
Place peppers on aluminium foil on a baking tray. Cook
15–20 minutes, turning halfway through, or until blackened
and blistered. Remove from heat. Place tea towel soaked in
cold water on top. Leave 5 minutes. Peel away skin with a
small knife.

2 Cut flesh into thin strips. Place on a platter. Drizzle
with combined oil and vinegar. Refrigerate, covered, 1 hour.
Add salt and pepper to taste before serving.

to prepare peppers

1 Place peppers on a
baking tray lined with
aluminium foil. Using a hot
grill or oven, cook 15–20
minutes, turning halfway,
or until the skin has
blackened and bubbled.

2 Place tea towel soaked in cold
water on top of peppers. Leave for
5 minutes. Peel away skin with a
small knife.

3 Or, remove peppers from
heat and immediately place
in a large freezer bag. Seal
bag. Place in a bowl of iced
water. Leave 2 minutes
before peeling.

Artichoke and radicchio salad

Artichokes have a wonderfully mellow flavour that's an excellent contrast with the sharpness of radiccio. Serve with lemon wedges and a few slivers of salty pecorino cheese.

4 small globe artichokes

1 clove garlic, thinly sliced

4 tablespoons olive oil

100ml dry white wine

salt and freshly ground black pepper

2 tablespoons balsamic vinegar

3 tablespoons fresh flat-leaved parsley,
    finely chopped

few sprigs lemon thyme, leaves
    finely chopped

2 medium heads treviso or round radicchio

80g pecorino

lemon wedges, to serve

serves **4**

preparation **10 minutes**

cooking **12 minutes**

- -

per serving 221 calories, 17g fat, 6g saturated fat,
4g carbohydrate, 3.5g sugar, 1g fibre, 0.4g salt

1 Prepare artichokes as in box below and cut each artichoke into four pieces.

2 Heat oil in a nonstick frying pan with a lid over medium heat. Add artichoke pieces and garlic. Cook, stirring, about 5 minutes. Add wine; season with salt and pepper. Cover pan and cook for about 6 minutes, or until artichokes are crisp-tender.

3 Using a slotted spoon, transfer artichokes to a plate. Leave to cool. Stir vinegar and herbs into pan juices. Cut radicchio into large pieces. Combine raddichio and pan juices and distribute among serving plates.

4 Using a vegetable peeler, slice pecorino into large, thin shavings. Arrange artichokes on top of radicchio. Scatter on pecorino. Serve with lemon wedges.

to trim artichokes

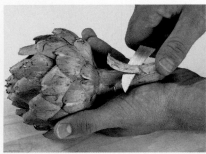

1 Cut off stalk, leaving a small length. Thinly slice skin from remaining stalk.

2 Trim tips of leaves with kitchen scissors. Remove the papery internal leaves.

3 Scrape out fibrous matter at base with a teaspoon. Wash artichoke bases to completely remove fibres.

Roast butternut and parmesan salad

Use either butternut squash or the scoopings from a Halloween pumpkin. Combine with shavings of Parmesan and a plentiful pile of rocket leaves for a delightful autumnal salad.

300g butternut squash or pumpkin,
   peeled and thinly sliced
5 tablespoons olive oil
1 tablespoon balsamic vinegar
salt and freshly ground black pepper
250g rocket
50g Parmesan

serves 4
preparation 15 minutes
cooking 30 minutes

- -

per serving 216 calories, 18g fat, 4.5g saturated fat,
8g carbohydrate, 5g sugar, 2g fibre, 0.3g salt

1 Heat oven to 180°C/gas 4. Toss squash or pumpkin with 1 tablespoon of the oil in a shallow baking dish. Cook 30 minutes, turning occasionally, or until golden brown. Set aside to cool a little.

2 Whisk vinegar and remaining 4 tablespoons oil until combined; season with salt and pepper to taste. Using a vegetable peeler, slice Parmesan into large, thin shavings.

3 Combine rocket and warm pumpkin in a serving bowl. Add vinaigrette and toss well. Top with Parmesan.

Rocket and radicchio salad with tomatoes

A side salad that packs plenty of punch – in terms of both looks and flavour. Pretty rocket and radiccio leaves balance the sweetness of cherry tomatoes while a little Parmesan and onion adds kick and salt.

250g cherry tomatoes

1 small onion

200g rocket

1 head treviso or round radicchio

4 tablespoons olive oil

3 tablespoons balsamic vinegar

1 clove garlic, crushed

salt and freshly ground black pepper

50g Parmesan

serves 4

preparation 20 minutes

per serving 192 calories, 15g fat, 4 g saturated fat, 7.5g carbohydrate, 6.4g sugar, 2g fibre, 0.3g salt

1 Cut tomatoes in half. Slice onion into thin rings. Layer rocket, radicchio, tomatoes and onion rings on a platter.

2 Whisk oil, vinegar and garlic until combined. Add salt and pepper to taste. Using a vegetable peeler, slice Parmesan into large, thin shavings.

3 Drizzle dressing over salad. Top with Parmesan.

treviso radicchio

Treviso is a type of radicchio that has long, narrow, pointed purple-tipped leaves that resemble chicory. It has a slightly less bitter taste than round radicchio.

Bavarian cabbage salad

Ultra-thin strips of cabbage, lots of fresh chives and tiny bits of bacon are dressed with wine vinegar and a few caraway seeds, then chilled for a super tasty side salad.

1kg tender green cabbage

salt

1 tablespoon caraway seeds

100g bacon, rind removed, finely diced

3 tablespoons vegetable oil

3 to 4 tablespoons white wine vinegar

freshly ground black pepper

1 teaspoon sugar

3 tablespoons chopped chives and
    a few whole chives, for garnish

serves 4

preparation + chilling 1 hour

cooking 10 minutes

----

per serving 190 calories, 11g fat, 2g saturated fat, 14g carbohydrate, 13g sugar, 5g fibre, 1.7g salt

1 Remove core from cabbage. Shred leaves finely with a knife or use a grater or mandoline.

2 Place 2 litres water in a large saucepan with 1 teaspoon salt and the caraway seeds. Bring to a boil. Add shredded cabbage; cook 2 minutes. Pour cabbage into a colander; refresh under cold running water. Leave to drain and cool completely.

3 Heat 1 tablespoon oil in a heavy-based pan over high heat. Add bacon and cook on all sides until crisp. Combine bacon and cabbage in a serving bowl.

4 Whisk remaining 2 tablespoons oil, vinegar, a little salt, pepper and the sugar in a bowl until well combined. Stir vinaigrette into salad. Place in refrigerator, covered, 45 minutes, to allow flavours to develop.

5 Just before serving, taste salad and adjust seasonings. Serve garnished with chopped and whole chives.

Fresh tomato salad

If you enjoy salsa, this salad is one for you. Chopped tomatoes, chillies, spring onion, coriander and mint are marinated in lime juice. Serve with tacos for a real Mexican touch.

3 medium tomatoes (about 500g)

4 spring onions, finely sliced

30g chopped fresh coriander leaves

3 tablespoons chopped fresh mint leaves

2 small red chillies, seeds removed, finely chopped

½ teaspoon ground coriander

½ teaspoon ground cumin

¼ cup lime juice

salt and freshly ground black pepper

serves 4

preparation + standing 40 minutes

---

per serving 25 calories, 0.5g fat, 0g saturated fat, 5g carbohydrate, 4.5g sugar, 1.5g fibre, trace salt

1 Cut tomatoes in half, remove seeds and dice flesh. Place in a serving bowl with spring onions, coriander, mint, chillies, ground coriander, cumin and lime juice. Stir to combine.

2 Leave for 30 minutes to allow the flavours to develop. Taste just before serving, adding salt and freshly ground black pepper to taste.

Watercress and baby spinach with goat's cheese

The peppery mustard-like taste of watercress and the sharpness of the goat's cheese give this attractive salad a full, bold flavour. It makes a good dinner party starter or a simple light lunch.

3 slices light rye bread, crusts removed
2 tablespoons butter
1 large clove garlic, halved lengthways
100g firm goat's cheese
100g watercress
100g baby spinach leaves
1 shallot, finely chopped
2 tablespoons olive oil
2 tablespoons balsamic vinegar
½ teaspoon Dijon mustard
salt and freshly ground black pepper

serves **4**

preparation **15 minutes**

cooking **15 minutes**

per serving 250 calories, 19g fat, 9g saturated fat, 12g carbohydrate, 3g sugar, 2g fibre, 0.9g salt

1 To make croutons, cut bread into small cubes. Melt about 1 ½ tablespoons butter in a nonstick frying pan over medium heat. Add garlic, sauté 2 minutes; discard. Add bread cubes; cook until golden brown on all sides, taking care butter does not burn. Set aside; keep warm.

2 Slice goat's cheese into four equal pieces. Heat remaining butter in a pan over medium heat. Add cheese; cook until it begins to melt and develops a golden-brown crust, about 4 minutes each side.

3 Divide watercress, spinach and shallot among serving plates. Whisk oil, vinegar, mustard, salt and pepper until combined. Drizzle over salad greens. Place a piece of goat's cheese on each plate and top with croutons.

cook's tip

Goat's cheese is made from pure goat's milk or a combination of goat's and cow's milk. Fresh goat's cheese has a creamy consistency and a mild, slightly tangy flavour. As it ages, goat's cheese hardens and the taste sharpens

health guide

Spinach contains many valuable nutrients such as antioxidants and bioflavonoids that help to block cancer-causing substances and processes.

Pak choi
with pan-fried tofu and peanuts

A type of Chinese cabbage that looks like a leafy green vegetable rather than a cabbage, pak choi is much richer in beta carotene and calcium than green cabbage. Peanuts and tofu add protein and there's heat from chilli with lime.

2 small heads baby pak choi

2 medium carrots

4 spring onions

200g firm tofu (smoked, if available)

2 small red chillies, or to taste

3 tablespoons groundnut oil

2 tablespoons lime juice

2 tablespoons soy sauce

¼ teaspoon ground ginger

¼ teaspoon lemon peel, grated

pinch of soft brown sugar

salt

3 tablespoons roasted peanuts

1 tablespoon finely chopped fresh coriander leaves, for garnish

serves **4**

preparation **20 minutes**

cooking **5 minutes**

per serving 231 calories, 17g fat, 3g saturated fat, 9g carbohydrate, 7g sugar, 3g fibre, 2g salt

1 Cut pak choi into thin strips. Score five narrow grooves lengthwise along each carrot. Slice carrots into thin rounds to create flower-shaped discs.

2 Finely dice white parts of spring onions. Cut green parts into thin rings. Distribute pak choi, carrots and spring onions among serving plates.

3 Cut tofu into small cubes. Halve chillies lengthways and discard seeds. Dice chillies finely.

4 Whisk 2 tablespoons of the peanut oil, all the lime juice, soy sauce, ground ginger, lemon peel, sugar and a little salt in a bowl until combined. Stir in chillies. Drizzle over salad.

5 Heat remaining 1 tablespoon oil in a nonstick frying pan over medium heat. Add tofu and fry until golden brown on all sides. Add peanuts and cook briefly, stirring. Add tofu and peanuts at once to salad. Sprinkle with coriander and serve.

health guide

Tofu, or bean curd, is made from soya beans. It is high in protein and is a good source of B vitamins. Tofu is available in firm, soft or silken textures and a variety of flavours, including smoked.

Asian bean sprout salad

Mung bean sprouts – which have a hint of sweetness – and peanuts add crunch to this sweet and sour salad. In Chinese medicine, mung beans are considered to be a yin or cooling food.

150g mung bean sprouts

2 spring onions, sliced into rounds

4 medium celery stalks, thinly sliced

1 medium mango or 2 small nectarines

½ small fresh pineapple (about 500g)

4 to 6 large Chinese cabbage leaves

4 tablespoons salted, roasted peanuts, coarsely chopped

spicy fruit dressing

2 tablespoons raspberry vinegar

3 tablespoons olive oil

4 tablespoons orange juice

¼ to ½ teaspoon sambal oelek (available in jars from Asian food shops and some supermarkets)

½ teaspoon ground ginger

¼ teaspoon finely grated lemon peel

serves 4

preparation 25 minutes

per serving 270 calories, 17g fat, 3g saturated fat, 24g carbohydrate, 22g sugar, 5g fibre, 0.2g salt

1 Combine sprouts, spring onions and celery in a large bowl. Peel mango and slice flesh thinly. Peel pineapple and cut into small chunks. Add to bowl.

2 To make spicy fruit dressing, whisk all the ingredients in a small bowl until combined. Stir into salad.

3 Cut Chinese cabbage leaves into wide strips. Distribute among serving plates. Add bean sprout salad and sprinkle with peanuts.

sambal oelek

A sambal is a fresh or cooked relish. Sambal oelek is a spicy relish which is often used in conjunction with other sambal ingredients. It is made from ground chillies, salt and vinegar or tamarind. Tamarind is a very acidic fruit which gives sambals a particularly sharp taste. In a traditional oelek, the chillies are not seeded, adding more heat.

Asian bean sprout salad

Sprouts salad with mushrooms and celery

✳ Slice **250g button mushrooms**. Slice **2 spring onions** and **4 medium celery stalks** as in the main recipe. Trim **150g mung bean sprouts**. Finely chop **1 clove garlic**.

✳ In a wok, heat **2 tablespoons oil** over medium heat. Cook mushrooms, spring onions and celery, stirring, 2 minutes. Add sprouts and garlic. Toss over high heat, 1 minute. Add **2 tablespoons each** of **rice vinegar** and **soy sauce**. Remove from heat. Season with salt to taste. Serve warm.

Mixed mushroom salad

An array of mushrooms including Portobello, oyster and nutty-tasting crisp-stemmed enoki mushrooms is roasted before serving with garlic, red onion, thyme and parsley.

about 700g button mushrooms, halved

150g Portobello or field or other brown-topped mushrooms, thickly sliced

150g oyster mushrooms, chopped

2 cloves garlic, crushed

1 tablespoon fresh thyme leaves

3 tablespoons olive oil

150g enoki mushrooms

1 medium red onion, sliced thinly

60g fresh parsley leaves, chopped

30g chives, chopped

2 tablespoons red wine vinegar

salt and freshly ground black pepper

serves 4

preparation 10 minutes

cooking 25 minutes

per serving 122 calories, 10g fat, 1.5g saturated fat, 3g carbohydrate, 2g sugar, 3.5g fibre, trace salt

1 Heat oven to 200°C / gas 6. Mix button, brown and oyster mushrooms with garlic and thyme in a roasting pan; drizzle with oil. Roast about 20 minutes or until tender. Add enoki mushrooms; roast another 5 minutes.

3 Place warm mushrooms in a large serving bowl; add onion, parsley, chives and vinegar. Add a little salt and a generous amount of pepper. Toss to combine.

mushrooms

Button mushrooms have a very mild flavour while oyster mushrooms have a very slight oyster taste that is enhanced with cooking. Enoki have a long, thin stem and a tiny button cup. They have a unique crunchy texture when eaten raw.

cook's tip

When cooking several varieties of mushrooms together, always add the enoki last because they need very little cooking. Freshly ground black pepper brings out the flavour of mushrooms, as does fresh thyme.

Tossed salad with pears and blue cheese

The soft sweetness of pears is complemented by the sharp, rich taste of blue cheese. Choose a variety of blue cheese that crumbles easily, such as Roquefort or Stilton.

2 pears, halved, cored and thinly sliced

185ml buttermilk

1 tablespoon white wine vinegar

salt and freshly ground black pepper

2 tablespoons chives, cut into short pieces

1 head butterhead lettuce

1 head radicchio or other red lettuce

75g watercress leaves

1 small cucumber, thinly sliced

2 tablespoons blue cheese, crumbled

serves 6

preparation 20 minutes

----

per serving 66 calories, 2g fat, 1g saturated fat, 0g carbohydrate, 8g sugar, 7.5g fibre, 0.2g salt

1 In a small bowl, toss pears with 2 tablespoons of the buttermilk to prevent flesh browning. Whisk the remaining buttermilk, the vinegar and a pinch each of salt and pepper in another small bowl until combined. Add chives.

2 Tear or chop leaves of both lettuces. Mix with watercress and cucumber. Arrange on serving plates and top with blue cheese and sliced pears. Drizzle a little buttermilk dressing over the top, serving the remainder separately.

cook's tip

Mesclun is a mixture of young salad leaves. The petals of edible flowers such as nasturtiums are sometimes included. Mesclun is sold loose or in packets from greengrocers and supermarkets. It's an easy, quick option when making a salad.

health guide

The darker the greens, the more nutritious the salad. Watercress and rocket, for instance, contain more beta carotene and vitamin C than the pale leaves of iceberg and butterhead lettuces.

Orange and asparagus salad

Choose the freshest ingredients you can for a super-easy, super-fast and super-delicious salad. Blanch the asparagus for just a minute, peel oranges and avocados, then lay on a bed of salad greens.

2 large oranges

about 250g thin asparagus spears

150g mixed salad greens

2 medium avocados, halved and sliced

orange mustard dressing

2 tablespoons orange juice

4 tablespoons olive oil

1 teaspoon Dijon mustard

salt and freshly ground black pepper

serves 4

preparation 20 minutes

cooking 1 minute

per serving 351 calories, 31g fat, 6g saturated fat, 13g carbohydrate, 11g sugar, 6.5g fibre, 0.2g salt

1 Peel oranges, remove all the white pith with a sharp knife and segment the flesh.

2 Bring a large saucepan of water to a boil; blanch asparagus 1 minute. Refresh under cold running water.

3 To make orange mustard dressing, whisk orange juice, oil, mustard, salt and pepper in a small bowl until combined.

4 Arrange salad greens on serving plates. Add orange segments, asparagus and avocado slices. Drizzle vinaigrette over the top and add a grinding of pepper.

Onion and tropical fruit salad

Sharpen up the warm, exotic flavours of mango and kiwifruit with a touch of red onion and a chilli and lime dressing, laced with chopped coriander.

1 medium red onion, sliced into thin rings

1 large, ripe but firm mango

2 kiwifruit, peeled and thinly sliced into rounds

1 small cucumber, thinly sliced

chilli lime dressing

1 fresh red chilli, seeded and finely chopped

2 tablespoons olive oil

2 tablespoons lime juice

1 teaspoon clear honey

2 tablespoons fresh coriander leaves, chopped

salt and freshly ground black pepper

serves 4

preparation + marinating 45 minutes

- -

per serving 103 calories, 6 g fat, 1g saturated fat, 12g carbohydrate, 11g sugar, 2 g fibre, trace salt

1 Slice onion rings in half. Place in a shallow dish. To make chilli lime dressing, combine all the dressing ingredients in a screw-top jar. Shake well to combine. Stir dressing into onion rings; marinate 30 minutes.

2 Slice flesh from mango, cutting down each side of the stone. Peel away skin and cut flesh into thin slices.

3 Add mango kiwifruit and cucumber to marinated onion and dressing. Combine gently to avoid breaking up the fruit.

mix and match

✳ If you find the taste of coriander too pungent, try using **choppec fresh mint.**

✳ Add **2 large, ripe, thinly sliced plums** to the salad and use **2 large segmented oranges** instead of the mango.

Citrus salad with goat's cheese

Citrus salad with goat's cheese

Citrus fruits, such as oranges and grapefruit, team well with salad greens and complement crunchy celery, carrots and walnuts. A little goat's cheese is mixed with lemon and orange juice in the dressing.

2 small oranges or 2 medium
   mandarins or tangerines
500g celery stalks, thinly sliced
2 medium carrots, coarsely grated
1 small red onion, finely diced
100g soft goat's cheese
3 tablespoons orange juice
2 tablespoons vegetable oil
1 tablespoon white wine vinegar
1 tablespoon lemon juice
salt and freshly ground black pepper
4 leaves each of treviso radicchio, cos
   and iceberg lettuce
55g pecans or walnuts

serves **4**

preparation **30 minutes**

-----

per serving 303 calories, 24g fat, 6g saturated fat,
14g carbohydrate, 12g sugar, 5g fibre, 0.6g salt

1 Peel and segment oranges. Cut in half crossways. Place in a bowl with celery, carrots and onion. Mix well.

2 Mash goat's cheese in a bowl with the orange juice. Stir in oil, vinegar and lemon juice. Add salt and pepper to taste. Spoon dressing over fruit and vegetables; mix gently.

3 To serve, place one leaf of each lettuce variety on each serving plate. Top with rest of salad. Garnish with nuts.

cook's tip

Buy nuts in small quantities and use them as soon as possible. If you have to store them, keep them in an airtight container in the refrigerator or freezer. The oil in nuts quickly turns rancid, particularly in a hot atmosphere.

Celery and apples with ricotta dressing

✳ In a serving bowl, combine **500g finely chopped celery**, **2 unpeeled tart red apples** cut into cubes and **2 finely sliced spring onions**.

✳ Combine **250g fresh ricotta**, **2 tablespoons olive oil**, **1 tablespoon lemon juice**, **1 teaspoon horseradish sauce**, **salt** and **freshly ground black pepper** in a small bowl. Stir into salad. Arrange **iceberg lettuce leaves** on serving plates and top with salad.

Radicchio and fennel salad with oranges

The pleasantly bitter taste of radicchio goes well with the aniseed flavour of fennel and the sweetness of oranges. Keep the leafy fennel fronds as a garnish.

1 large head treviso radicchio

2 large oranges

1 large or 2 small fennel heads (about 1kg total) with leafy fronds

2 small white onions

4 tablespoons olive oil

1 tablespoon white wine vinegar

1 tablespoon lemon juice

1 sprig rosemary, leaves finely chopped

salt and freshly ground black pepper

120g pitted black olives

serves 4

preparation 25 minutes

per serving 232 calories, 16g fat, 2g saturated fat, 17g carbohydrate, 15g sugar, 10g fibre, 0.9g salt

1 Line individual plates with radicchio leaves. Peel and segment oranges.

2 Using a vegetable peeler, slice fennel head into thin strips. Slice onions into thin rings.

3 Whisk oil, vinegar, lemon juice and rosemary in a bowl until combined. Season with salt and pepper to taste.

4 Finely chop a few fennel fronds. Layer fennel, oranges and onions onto radicchio. Drizzle with vinaigrette. Top with fennel fronds and olives.

cook's tip

The salad looks very attractive if the fennel heads are cut into thin slices lengthways using a vegetable peeler. Trim the stalk so that a small amount remains. This way, the individual layers of fennel will not fall apart during slicing.

Sugar-snap peas with grapes and feta

A great summer salad pairs crisp sugar-snap pea pods with plenty of rocket plus the contrasting texture and flavour of grapes, feta cheese and tomatoes.

grated peel and juice of 1 small lemon
½ teaspoon caster sugar
½ teaspoon Dijon mustard
salt and freshly ground black pepper
1 tablespoon olive oil
300g sugar–snap peas
250g seedless black grapes, halved
250g feta cheese, thinly sliced
50g rocket, shredded
175g baby spinach leaves

serves 4
preparation 15 minutes
cooking 2 minutes

per serving 260 calories, 16g fat, 9g saturated fat, 16g carbohydrate, 14g sugar, 2.5g fibre, 2.4 salt

1 Place lemon peel, juice, sugar, mustard and a generous seasoning of salt and pepper in a serving bowl. Whisk until sugar and salt have dissolved completely. Whisk in oil.

2 Cut sugar-snap peas in half crossways, leaving a few small ones whole. Bring a large saucepan of water to a boil. Add sugar-snaps and bring water back to a boil. Drain sugar-snaps immediately and refresh under cold running water. Add to serving bowl. Turn to coat with dressing.

3 Add grapes, feta, rocket and spinach. Mix again gently to coat with dressing.

Sugar-snap peas

Sugar-snap peas, like mangetout are eaten pods and all. They have a sweet taste and tender texture. They are a good source of dietary fibre and vitamin C.

Fruity salad with blue cheese dressing

✳ Crumble or chop **60g Danish blue cheese** in a serving bowl. Mix with **1 tablespoon apple cider vinegar** and **2 tablespoons olive oil**.

✳ Halve and core **2 ripe but firm pears**, then slice thinly. Add to bowl; toss to coat with dressing. Add **250g halved seedless black grapes** and mix well. Add a **handful of watercress sprigs, 250g baby spinach leaves** and **2 tablespoons chopped walnuts**. Toss to combine.

Sugar-snap salad with grapes and feta

Red cabbage with citrus

Teaming red cabbage with sweet ingredients – traditionally with apples in a cooked dish, here with oranges and mandarins – is a classic feature of Central European cooking.

1 small red cabbage (about 750g)
1 teaspoon salt
2 medium oranges
3 small mandarins or tangerines
3 tablespoons walnut oil
2 to 3 tablespoons red wine vinegar
freshly ground black pepper
55g walnuts, coarsely chopped

serves 4
preparation 35 minutes

per serving 251 calories, 18g fat, 2g saturated fat, 17g carbohydrate, 15g sugar, 7g fibre, 1g salt

1 Discard thick outer leaves of cabbage. Cut cabbage into quarters. Remove core and slice cabbage thinly. Place in a serving bowl.

2 Sprinkle cabbage with salt. Knead firmly by hand for about 5 minutes; the cabbage will soften slightly and become milder in flavour. Leave 15 minutes. Place in a colander. Rinse under cold running water; drain.

3 Peel and segment oranges and mandarins. Cut into small pieces over a bowl to catch the juices; discard seeds. Combine fruit and cabbage.

4 Whisk reserved citrus juice, oil, vinegar and pepper until combined. Stir into salad. Top with walnuts.

cook's tip

Walnut oil has a distinctive flavour that is delicious with the walnuts in this recipe. Like nuts, oils made from nuts quickly turn rancid in a warm temperature. Buy in small amounts and store in a cool place.

health guide

Cabbage is a source of vitamin C, carotenoids and folate and is high in fibre. It is thought to help fight against hormone-related cancers. Red cabbage is higher in vitamin C than green.

Red cabbage with citrus

Red cabbage with port vinaigrette

* Quarter and thinly slice **1 small red cabbage**. Bring **150ml water** to a boil in a large saucepan with **3 tablespoons red wine vinegar**, **1 teaspoon salt** and **2 cloves**. Add cabbage, cover and cook for 20 to 25 minutes until crisp-tender, stirring occasionally. Transfer to a colander. Drain and let cool.

* Combine **2 tablespoons port**, **1 tablespoon red wine vinegar**, **1 tablespoon cranberry sauce**, **1 tablespoon orange marmalade**, **2 tablespoons walnut oil** and a pinch of salt. Stir into cabbage. Chill, covered, 2 hours.

Roasted beetroot and orange

Tender, baby beetroots home-roasted with garlic and olive oil have a subtle sweet taste that's a far cry from the vinegary globes that you can buy ready-prepared from supermarkets.

800g baby beetroot, trimmed and scrubbed

3 cloves garlic, peeled, flattened with the back of a knife

2 tablespoons olive oil

1 large orange

100g black olives

1 small red onion, thinly sliced

250g rocket

2 teaspoons red wine vinegar

1 teaspoon wholegrain mustard

salt and freshly ground black pepper

serves 4

preparation 10 minutes

cooking 45 minutes

per serving 193 calories, 10g fat, 1.5g saturated fat, 22g carbohydrate, 19g sugar, 6g fibre, 1g salt

1 Heat oven to 180°C/gas 4. Combine beetroot, garlic and oil in a baking dish. Cover with aluminium foil and roast 45 minutes or until beetroot is tender. Remove beetroots from dish; reserve pan juices.

2 Cut beetroot into quarters. Peel and segment orange. Place in a serving bowl with the olives, onion and rocket.

3 Combine vinegar, mustard and reserved pan juices in a small bowl. Season to taste with salt and pepper. Stir into salad just before serving.

health guide

Oranges are a low GI food. They are ideal for people with diabetes and for anyone needing an energy boost. They are high in vitamin C, which may reduce the risk of strokes and some cancers.

cook's tip

Purchase fresh beetroot with crisp, bright green leafy tops. Scatter raw leaves on salads or cook them as for spinach. They are rich in beta carotene.

Crunchy salad with apples

The radish and apples give this salad a satisfying crunch. There's no need to peel the apples; their skin contains beneficial nutrients.

2 tablespoons sunflower seeds

1 small head cos lettuce or other crisp lettuce

2 medium tart apples (about 300g)

1 tablespoon lemon juice

1 small black radish or young turnip (about 100g)

alfalfa sprouts or trimmed salad cress, to garnish

cider vinegar dressing

125g soured cream

1 tablespoon apple cider vinegar

2 tablespoons vegetable oil

pinch of sugar

salt and freshly ground black pepper

serves 4

preparation 15 minutes

cooking 2 to 3 minutes

per serving 200 calories, 16.5g fat, 5g saturated fat, 11.5g carbohydrate, 10g sugar, 2.5g fibre, trace salt

1 Dry-roast sunflower seeds in a heavy pan over medium heat until light brown. Stir constantly, taking care seeds do not burn. Transfer to a plate and leave to cool.

2 Reserve a few whole lettuce leaves and tear or cut the rest into strips. Cut apples into small pieces and place in a bowl with lemon juice to prevent discolouration. Peel radish or turnip and grate finely.

3 To make cider vinegar dressing, whisk soured cream, vinegar, oil and sugar in a large bowl. Add salt and pepper to taste. Add torn lettuce and apples. Stir gently to combine.

4 Place whole lettuce leaves on serving plate. Top with salad. Sprinkle with sunflower seeds, radish and sprouts.

apples

For apples that will be used unpeeled wash and wipe them thoroughly to get rid of any pesticide residues. Biting and chewing an apple stimulates the gums. The sweetness of the apple encourages an increased flow of saliva, which helps to reduce tooth decay by lowering bacteria levels in the mouth.

Salad greens with fresh figs

Make the most of perfectly ripe figs when they're in season. They taste superb when accompanied by a blue cheese, here represented in a dressing that's laced with either Gorgonzola or dolcelatte.

50g baby spinach leaves

100g lamb's lettuce

100g frisée lettuce

4 tablespoons coarsely chopped walnuts

4 large fresh figs

blue cheese dressing

50g soft blue cheese, such as
  Gorgonzola or dolcelatte

2 tablespoons light soured cream

1 tablespoon walnut oil

1½ tablespoons white wine vinegar

2 tablespoons apple juice

pinch of sugar

salt and freshly ground black pepper

serves 4

preparation 25 minutes

----

per serving 223 calories, 18g fat, 4.5g saturated fat, 11g carbohydrate, 10g sugar, 2.4g fibre, 0.6g salt

1 Distribute spinach, lamb's lettuce and frisée among individual serving plates.

2 Trim stem ends from figs. Cut each fig into eight pieces and arrange on top of salad greens.

3 To make blue cheese dressing, mash cheese in a bowl with sour cream. Gradually stir in walnut oil, vinegar, apple juice and sugar until well combined. Add salt and pepper to taste. Spoon over salad and sprinkle with walnuts.

cook's tip

Choose unbruised figs that are soft but not mushy. Ripe figs may be eaten unpeeled. As they ripen, they become increasingly aromatic and sweet. Figs are a good source of iron, potassium and fibre.

Mushroom salad with goat's cheese dressing

✴ Prepare **salad greens** as for main recipe. Slice **250g large mushrooms**. Melt **2 tablespoons butter** in a frying pan over medium heat. Add mushrooms. Cook until all the liquid has evaporated, about 10 minutes. Season with **salt, pepper** and **½ teaspoon dried mixed herbs**.

✴ Mix **120g soft goat's cheese** or other creamy cheese, **3 tablespoons yoghurt**, **1 tablespoon olive oil** and **1 tablespoon lemon juice**. Add salt and pepper to taste. Mix with salad greens. Arrange salad on a serving plate. Top with hot mushrooms.

Salad greens with fresh figs

Cabbage and nectarines with yoghurt chutney

Sprinkle nutty dry-roasted pumpkin seeds over thinly sliced nectarines and Chinese cabbage, then add an unusual yoghurt chutney dressing for a little extra spice.

4 tablespoons shelled pumpkin seeds

1 small head Chinese cabbage (about 500g)

1 large head chicory

3 medium fully ripe nectarines

yoghurt chutney

juice of 1 medium lemon

2 tablespoons olive oil

125g yoghurt

2 teaspoons mango chutney, plus more
   as needed

salt and freshly ground black pepper

¼ teaspoon mild or hot curry powder,
   plus more as needed

serves 4

preparation 20 minutes

cooking 4 minutes

per serving 213 calories, 14g fat, 2.5g saturated fat, 15g carbohydrate, 12g sugar, 3.5g fibre, 0.2g salt

1 Dry-roast pumpkin seeds in a heavy pan over medium heat for 3 to 4 minutes. Stir constantly, taking care seeds do not burn. Transfer to a plate and leave to cool.

2 Cut cabbage and chicory into thin strips. Use to line a serving platter. Halve nectarines. Slice flesh thinly. Drizzle with a little lemon juice to prevent discolouration.

3 To make yoghurt chutney, combine remaining lemon juice, oil, yoghurt and chutney. Add salt, pepper and curry powder to taste. Add more chutney to taste.

4 Spoon a little dressing over the salad. Serve the rest separately with a little curry powder sprinkled on top. Place nectarines on top of salad. Sprinkle with pumpkin seeds.

chutney

In India, a chutney is often made to be eaten fresh, using whatever suitable full-flavoured fruit or vegetable ingredients are locally traditional or available. Chutneys fulfil a similar role to the salsas of Mexican cooking and European relishes. They range from mildly spicy to hot, with a variety of seasonings added.

cook's tip

If nectarines are not in season, slices of peach or mango may be used instead, or combined if you like.

Cabbage and nectarines with yoghurt chutney

Spicy chinese cabbage salad

✳ Finely slice **500g Chinese cabbage**. Slice **3 spring onions** into rings. Halve **1 red** and **1 yellow pepper**, discard seeds and cut into strips. Mix all ingredients in a bowl.

✳ Make a vinaigrette with **3 tablespoons tomato juice**, **1 clove crushed garlic**, **3 tablespoons olive oil**, **2 tablespoons balsamic vinegar**, salt, freshly ground black pepper and **sambal oelek** to taste. Stir into salad. Serve with **toasted sourdough bread** and wedges of mature, **strong-flavoured cheddar**.

Rice, Pasta, Bean & Grain Salads

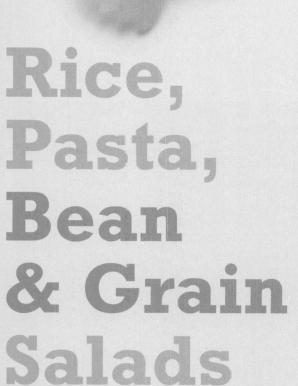

For an easy way to turn a lightweight salad into a substantial main course, add some rice, pasta, beans or grains that add fibre, protein and starchy carbohydrates to the diet. Versatile and inexpensive, the mild taste and interesting textures of these items team well with virtually all other kinds of salad ingredients.

Rice, pasta, beans & grains at a glance

Versatile, inexpensive and with a long shelf-life, these versatile ingredients are an essential in every storecupboard. The many varieties of rice, pasta, beans and grains available in dried or canned form all add texture to salads and absorb the flavours of other ingredients well. They transform a salad into a substantial main meal and help to make a small amount go a long way. And rice, pasta, beans and grains have even more to recommend them. They each contain valuable nutrients that are beneficial to your general health and help to fight specific health problems.

Pasta and noodles

Both fresh and dried pasta have the same nutritional benefits. Oriental noodles can be used in salads in the same way as Italian pasta. Although pasta itself is low in salt and fat, some sauces and dressings used in pasta salads are high in these ingredients. If you are concerned about your intake, be judicious in the amount of sauce or dressing used, or, replace ingredients such as full-fat cream, soured cream and other rich dairy products with their low-fat or light counterparts. Salty condiments such as soy sauce can be replaced with a low-salt variety or herbs.

conchiglie (shells)

farfalle (bow-ties)

fettuccine

fusilli (spirals)

penne (quills)

rigatoni

tortellini

rice noodles

Rice

Rice is gluten-free, easy to digest and rarely, if ever, causes allergies. It provides complex or starchy carbohydrate and some B vitamins. Rice can be cooked by boiling (in stock or water), microwaving or steaming. Cooked cold rice is quickly reheated by steaming or microwaving.

Of the many hundreds of different varieties grown, some are used only in their country of origin; others are widely available. The types used in this book are either long-grain or medium-grain. Long-grain basmati has a beautiful nutty taste and aroma that goes well with all kinds of ingredients, especially those spicy flavours. The medium-length rice used is the Italian arborio, which absorbs a large volume of liquid during cooking and tastes creamy when cooked, yet still retains its firmness.

'Rice...is beautiful when it grows, precision rows of sparkling green stalks shooting up to reach the hot summer sun...'

Shizuo Tsuji
Japanese food expert

rice check

❋ Rice is surprisingly high in calories, so it's best to keep portions small.

❋ Rice is highly digestible and contains only a trace of fat and virtually no salt.

❋ Store cooked rice in a sealed container in the refrigerator for a day only as it can harbour harmful bacteria. Cooked rice freezes well.

❋ Wild rice can be expensive. Combine it with other types to minimise cost.

brown rice

Brown rice has a much higher fibre content than white rice and a higher nutrient content. It takes longer to cook than white and has a nutty taste.

long-grain white rice

The milling process removes the bran and germ from brown rice to produce white. Hence, although it is still a source of energy, white rice has less nutritional value and fibre content than brown. The grains remain separate when cooked and the finished result is fairly dry and firm.

wild rice

This is an aquatic grass and not a true rice. Wild rice is high in protein and fibre and several B vitamins. Cooked, it swells to up to four times its original volume. The grain splits to reveal a fluffy white interior. It has a nutty taste and is good combined with fluffy white rice.

Beans

Canned and dried beans are rich in health-protecting antioxidants. They provide useful amounts of fibre, protein, iron and zinc. Soluble fibre slows the digestion, leading to a slow, steady blood-sugar rise rather than a spike. The protein does not raise blood sugar levels and it helps the body process carbohydrates in a meal more efficiently. The salt content of canned beans can sometimes be high. Reduce the amount by rinsing the beans in cold water before use.

butter beans

Starchy and filling, butter beans come in two sizes; a large variety and the smaller lima beans. They are popular in soups and dishes such as the French cassoulet but also make an excellent salad ingredient with other beans and a range of other ingredients.

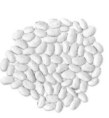

broad (fava) beans

These large, flat, beans – brown when dried – with an earthy flavour are often used in Mediterranean and Middle Eastern salads. Use them with ingredients that have a robust flavour, such as spices or smoked meat and fish.

bean check

* Beans and rice together make a complete protein. On their own, each lacks certain amino acids, the building blocks of protein.

* For dried beans, soaking and cooking times vary depending on the type used. As a general rule, soak the beans in cold water for 12 hours or overnight. Drain and rinse. Place in a saucepan. Add water or stock to cover. Simmer for up to 2 hours. Top up the liquid, as needed.

cannellini

This variety of haricot bean is widely grown in Italy. Cannellini beans have a mild taste that absorbs other flavours well. Use them is Tuscan-style salads that include canned or fresh tuna or hard-boiled eggs or marinated artichoke hearts.

chickpeas

Chickpeas have a nutty taste. They are richer in vitamin E than most other beans. They are often used in East Mediterranean, Indian and North African cooking.

kidney beans

Pink or red kidney-shaped beans have meaty white flesh and a pronounced flavour. They retain their colour on cooking and look most attractive combined with other colourful ingredients in salads. Their flavour and texture work especially well in salads that include white rice.

lentils

Whatever their colour (brown, orange, green or yellow), lentils are rich in protein and high in fibre. Like other grains, they're an excellent meat substitute. Unlike other dried beans, they do not need to be soaked overnight. Lentils feature in Middle Eastern and Central European cuisines and go well with spices.

Grains

Like uncooked rice, pasta and beans, grains are best stored in a cool, dry place. They have a long shelf-life, but keep an eye on their use-by date. Check unsprayed organic grains regularly because they can attract weevils and other food pests.

Whole grains are rich in fibre and complex carbohydrates as well as many vitamins and minerals. They are low in fat and some have the added advantage of being gluten-free.

buckwheat

Buckwheat was first grown thousands of years ago in China and Japan. It isn't, in fact, a cereal grain, but is the seed of a plant that belongs to the same family as dock and sorrel. It is also closely related to the rhubarb family. The seeds look like grains and can be cooked in the same way. Buckwheat provides useful amounts of minerals, vitamin B, potassium, phosphorus and dietary fibre. Kasha is the name frequently given to whole buckwheat grains (often cracked) that have been toasted or roasted.

bulgur wheat

Originating from the Persian word meaning 'bruised grain', bulgur is made of wheat that has been boiled, dried, hulled and shredded. Bulgur has a nutty and slightly savoury taste. Although it is often referred to as cracked wheat, it has had the bran removed, which cracked wheat still retains. (Cracked wheat is also known as kibbled wheat.) Bulgur is available ground to fine, medium or coarse granules. Soak grains in hot water for 15 to 20 minutes, until the water is absorbed and the grains have expanded and become fluffy. With its golden hue and pronounced nutty flavour, bulgur is a delicious addition to Middle Eastern dishes. It is best known in tabbouleh, a salad containing tomatoes, onions, parsley and mint.

couscous

It is hard to imagine North African cooking without the addition of couscous. Couscous is coarse-ground wheat made into tiny balls and pre-cooked. Preparing 'real' couscous is quite time-consuming; fortunately, there are some good-quality instant varieties on the market. To prepare them, add boiling water or stock and then leave to stand for a few minutes before stirring in a little butter and fluffing up the grains with a fork. Couscous is best used in Moroccan and Mediterranean-style salads with strongly flavoured ingredients.

quinoa

Pronounced 'keen-wah', this small grain originally came from the Andes in South America. It can be used like brown rice in salads but has a slightly sweeter taste. The small, round grains contain many valuable nutrients. Used in a salad, boiled quinoa grains taste best with green vegetables and light vinaigrettes, but also team well with peppers, sweetcorn or ham. Quinoa has the added healthy advantage that it is gluten-free.

grain check

* Buckwheat, maize, millet and quinoa are all gluten-free.

* Grains are low in fat. When eaten with canned or dried beans, they are a good source of complete protein.

* Research indicates that eating larger quantities of whole grains may significantly reduce the risk of developing type 2 diabetes and heart disease. There is growing evidence that eating whole grains instead of refined varieties can also help to reduce the risk of developing certain types of cancers.

Pasta salad with peas and ham

You can use any kind of pasta shapes but ideally, choose one that will hold the mayonnaise well, such as fusilli (spirals) or farfalle (bow-tie pasta). This is an excellent salad for a packed lunch.

300g fusilli (spiral pasta)
240g frozen peas
300g ham, in one piece
10 small gherkins in vinegar, finely diced
3 medium tomatoes, halved and sliced
few sprigs of parsley

yoghurt mayonnaise

125g yoghurt
125ml light mayonnaise
2 tablespoons white wine vinegar
salt and freshly ground black pepper
40g chopped fresh parsley

serves 4

preparation + chilling 1 hour

cooking 15 minutes

----

per serving 509 calories, 15g fat, 3g saturated fat, 68g carbohydrate, 9g sugar, 6g fibre, 3g salt

1 Cook pasta in plenty of lightly salted boiling water until *al dente*, following packet instructions. Drain, rinse under cold running water and leave to cool. Cook peas in lightly salted water 2 to 3 minutes; leave to cool in cooking water.

2 Strain peas, reserving cooking water. Cut ham into small cubes. Combine pasta, peas, ham and gherkins in a serving bowl; mix well.

3 To make yoghurt mayonnaise, whisk yoghurt, mayonnaise, 4 tablespoons reserved cooking water and vinegar in a bowl until creamy and well combined. Season generously with salt and pepper. Stir in chopped parsley.

4 Stir dressing into salad. Chill, covered, 30 minutes. Garnish with tomatoes and parsley sprigs.

Pasta salad with green vegetables

* Cook **300g farfalle (bow-tie pasta)** as for main recipe. Finely dice **2 shallots.** Thinly slice **2 courgettes.**

* Heat **3 tablespoons olive oil** in nonstick pan. Add shallots; cook until transparent. Add courgettes, **250g fresh or frozen broad or lima beans** and **125ml vegetable stock.** Cover; cook over medium heat 10 minutes. Drain; cool. Combine vegetables and pasta in a bowl. Whisk **½ teaspoon cayenne pepper, 1 teaspoon ground cumin** and **1 tablespoon lemon juice.** Add **salt** to taste. Stir into salad. Chill.

**Pasta salad
with peas and ham**

Asparagus and fettucine

You can use most kinds of thin, cured ham in this recipe. It can also be made with white asparagus if you can find it in season. Remember that it needs peeling completely and takes longer to cook than green.

300g fettuccine

500g medium to thick asparagus spears

2 tablespoons olive oil

1 tablespoon lemon–flavoured olive oil

2 tablespoons balsamic vinegar

salt and freshly ground black pepper

150g fresh ricotta

3 to 4 tablespoons milk

1 tablespoon lemon juice

4 tablespoons Parmesan, freshly grated

100g Parma ham or other prosciutto

fresh basil leaves, for garnish

serves 4

preparation 15 minutes

cooking 15 minutes

------

per serving 550 calories, 22g fat, 8g saturated fat, 62g carbohydrate, 7g sugar, 4.5g fibre, 0.6g salt

1 Cook pasta in plenty of lightly salted boiling water until *al dente*, following packet instructions. Drain, rinse under cold running water and leave to cool. Trim ends from asparagus spears. Peel white asparagus completely and green asparagus only at the ends.

2 Using a sharp knife or vegetable peeler, slice asparagus lengthways into thin strips. Place in a steamer basket. Fill a large saucepan with water to a depth equal to the width of two fingers; bring to a boil. Reduce heat to a simmer. Place steamer basket on top of pan. Cover; cook asparagus about 5 minutes (green); 10 minutes (white) or until crisp-tender. Drain, reserving cooking water. Leave to cool.

3 Whisk olive oil, lemon-flavoured olive oil, vinegar and 4 to 5 tablespoons reserved cooking water in a large bowl until combined. Add salt and pepper to taste. Add pasta; stir to coat with dressing. Stir in asparagus.

4 Combine ricotta, milk and lemon juice. Stir in Parmesan; add salt and pepper to taste. Trim fat from ham. Cut ham into narrow strips. Arrange salad in individual bowls. Spoon a little ricotta mixture on each serving. Add ham. Garnish with basil leaves.

health guide

Pasta is low in fat and sodium. Adding salt to the water when cooking pasta is not essential; you will still get a good result without it.

Farfalle salad with chicken

Cook sliced courgettes that have been briefly marinated in rosemary, garlic and oil; stir-fry thin strips of chicken, then serve with pasta bows, rocket and a plenty of herbs.

250g farfalle (bow-tie pasta)
4 medium courgettes (about 400g)
1 sprig fresh rosemary
1 clove garlic, finely chopped
4 tablespoons olive oil
salt and freshly ground black pepper
175g rocket
175g cherry tomatoes, halved
3 tablespoons balsamic vinegar
3 sprigs each of fresh marjoram, thyme
    and flat-leaved parsley
2 tablespoons vegetable oil
400g skinless chicken breast fillets,
    sliced into thin, even strips
1 tablespoon lemon juice

serves 4

preparation 20 minutes

cooking 20 minutes

per serving 564 calories, 22g fat, 4g saturated fat, 54g carbohydrate, 7g sugar, 4g fibre, 0.2g salt

1 Cook pasta in plenty of lightly salted boiling water until *al dente*, following packet instructions. Drain, rinse under cold running water and leave to cool. Cut courgettes into rounds. Roughly chop rosemary leaves. Combine courgettes, rosemary, garlic and 2 tablespoons olive oil in a bowl and leave for a few minutes.

2 Heat a nonstick pan over medium heat. Add the courgette mixture and cook until courgettes are golden brown. Sprinkle with salt and pepper and transfer to a large bowl with the pasta. Add rocket and tomatoes. Stir gently to combine.

3 Whisk vinegar, remaining 2 tablespoons olive oil, salt and pepper in a bowl until combined. Stir into salad.

4 Finely chop leaves of all the herbs. Heat vegetable oil in a nonstick pan over high heat and stir-fry chicken until golden brown. Season with salt and pepper.

5 Distribute pasta salad among serving bowls. Top with chicken and herbs and drizzle with lemon juice.

Mixed salad with chicken and spicy dressing

✳ Coarsely grate **2 carrots**. Roughly chop **3 celery stalks**. Finely slice **3 spring onions**. Arrange leaves of **1 head iceberg lettuce** on a serving platter and top with vegetables.

✳ Whisk **2 tablespoons lime juice**, **4 tablespoons olive oil**, **1 tablespoon white wine vinegar**, **1 teaspoon ground ginger**, **1 teaspoon sugar** and **salt**, **pepper** and **sambal oelek (Indonesian chilli paste)** to taste in a small bowl. Stir into salad.

✳ Cut **500g chicken breast fillets** into strips. Stir-fry in **vegetable oil** until golden brown. Drizzle with **1 tablespoon lime juice**. Add to salad.

Farfalle salad with chicken

Green pasta salad

Pasta is now available in many colours, including green, red, yellow and even black – from squid ink. Green pasta gets its colour either from basil or spinach.

500g green fettuccine

250g cherry tomatoes

2 small Mediterranean cucumbers

250g rocket

1 medium red onion, finely sliced

250g baby mozzarella balls

black olives for garnish

basil pesto

60g fresh basil leaves

2 cloves garlic, roughly chopped

1 tablespoon pine nuts

4 tablespoons grated pecorino

6 tablespoons olive oil

3 tablespoons lemon juice

2 tablespoons vegetable stock (broth)

salt and freshly ground black pepper

serves 6

preparation 20 minutes

cooking 10 minutes

per serving 578 calories, 26g fat, 10g saturated fat, 67g carbohydrate, 5g sugar, 4g fibre, 0.6g salt

1 Cook pasta in plenty of lightly salted boiling water until *al dente*, following packet instructions. Drain, rinse under cold running water and leave to cool. Cut tomatoes in half. Slice cucumbers in half lengthways and slice thinly.

2 Combine tomatoes, cucumbers, rocket, onion and pasta in a large bowl. Drain mozzarella and mix into the salad.

3 To make basil pesto, clean leaves by wiping them with paper towel; do not wash. Combine basil, garlic, pine nuts and pecorino in a food processor and process finely. Combine oil, lemon juice and stock in a small bowl and add to mixture in a steady stream with the motor running until amalgamated. Add salt and pepper to taste.

4 Stir basil pesto into salad or serve separately. Spoon salad into individual bowls and garnish with olives.

cook's tip

Pesto may be also made with a mixture of equal amounts of basil and fresh parsley leaves. An alternative is to use equal amounts of fresh coriander and parsley leaves.

Orecchiette salad with tuna and aioli

This substantial salad has two dressings: a herby vinaigrette and a freshly made aioli (creamy garlic sauce). You could use chunks of grilled tuna instead of canned.

350g orecchiette ('little ears' pasta)

250g fresh asparagus spears

1 medium courgette

1 medium orange pepper

1 can (180g) tuna in water, drained

1 cup (120g) pitted green olives

herb vinaigrette

2 tablespoons red wine vinegar

2 tablespoons sunflower oil

salt and freshly ground black pepper

1 teaspoon dried mixed herbs

aioli

2 cloves garlic

½ teaspoon salt

1 egg yolk

1 tablespoon white wine vinegar

125ml olive oil

1 tablespoon lemon juice

freshly ground black pepper

serves 4

preparation 20 minutes

cooking 8 minutes

per serving 700 calories, 37g fat, 5.5g saturated fat, 70g carbohydrate, 6g sugar, 5g fibre, 1.1g salt

1 Cook pasta in plenty of lightly salted boiling water until *al dente*, following packet instructions. Drain, rinse under cold running water and leave to cool. Trim asparagus and cut into small pieces. Place in a steamer basket. Fill a large saucepan with water to a depth equal to the width of two fingers; bring to a boil. Reduce heat to a simmer. Place steamer basket on top of pan. Cover; cook asparagus 6 to 8 minutes. Leave to cool.

2 Slice courgette into rounds. Cut pepper in half and chop into small pieces. Separate tuna into flakes with a fork. Finely chop olives.

3 To make herb vinaigrette, whisk all the ingredients in a large bowl until combined. Add pasta, asparagus, courgette, pepper and olives.

4 To make aioli, all ingredients should be at room temperature to avoid curdling. Mash garlic and salt to a fine paste in a bowl. Using an hand mixer or a whisk, beat in egg yolk and ½ tablespoon vinegar until creamy. Add oil, drop by drop at first, then in a steady stream. Beat until mixture is thick and creamy. Season well with remaining ½ tablespoon vinegar, lemon juice and salt and pepper to taste.

5 Distribute salad among serving bowls and add tuna. Spoon a little aioli on top. Serve remainder on the side.

health guide

Buy canned tuna that is packed in water. Tuna packed in oil is higher in calories. If you do choose to use it, drain it well to remove as much of the oil as possible.

Pasta vegetable salad in pepper halves

This is a salad variation on stuffed peppers: here they're left uncooked and filled with macaroni, sweetcorn, gherkins and chunks of Cheddar or Emmental cheese in a creamy dressing.

250g macaroni

1 medium green pepper

2 medium red and 2 medium yellow peppers

150g Cheddar or Emmental cheese

90g drained canned, or frozen and defrosted, sweetcorn

4 small gherkins in vinegar, finely diced

1 medium onion, finely diced

30g fresh basil, chopped

cream dressing

2 tablespoons olive oil

2 tablespoons white wine vinegar

1 tablespoon lemon juice

125g double cream

herb salt and freshly ground black pepper

serves 4

preparation 30 minutes

cooking 10 minutes

----

per serving 603 calories, 33g fat, 17g saturated fat, 62g carbohydrate, 11g sugar, 4g fibre, 0.9g salt

1 Cook pasta in plenty of lightly salted boiling water until *al dente*, following packet instructions. Drain, rinse under cold running water and leave to cool.

2 Halve green pepper and cut into small pieces. Halve red and yellow peppers without removing stalks; discard seeds. Cut cheese into small cubes.

3 To make cream dressing, whisk oil, vinegar, lemon juice and cream in a large bowl until combined. Add herb salt and pepper to taste. Add pasta, sweetcorn, gherkins, onion and pepper pieces and stir to combine. Taste and add more seasoning, as needed. Spoon salad mixture into pepper halves. Top with cheese. Sprinkle with chopped basil.

raw capsicums

Raw peppers are rich in vitamin C. Red ones contain the highest amount. Store peppers in a cool, dark place and use them within a few days. The vitamin content declines the longer that the capsicums are kept.

**Pasta vegetable salad
in pepper halves**

Pasta salad with grilled peppers

✳ Cook **500g farfalle (bow-tie pasta)** as for main recipe. Leave to cool. Roast **6 red peppers** in a preheated 240°C/gas 9 oven until skin blisters. Remove from oven, cover with a wet tea towel and leave 5 minutes. Peel off skin. Cut peppers into small pieces.

✳ Whisk **4 tablespoons olive oil, 2 tablespoons white wine vinegar, 2 tablespoons lemon juice, ½ teaspoon Dijon mustard** and **1 clove garlic, finely chopped,** until combined. Add **salt** and **pepper** to taste. Mix all ingredients in a serving bowl. Sprinkle with finely chopped fresh parsley.

Farfalle salad with beans and ham

Vary this simple, economical recipe depending on what you have available in the fridge. Use smoked chicken or turkey or a combination of spicy cooked chorizo, salami and ham.

300g farfalle (bow–tie pasta)

400g fresh green beans, trimmed

6 sprigs thyme

½ teaspoon salt

250g ham, in one piece

2 shallots, finely diced

4 large red radishes, cut into quarters, for garnish

paprika soured cream dressing

200g light soured cream

1 tablespoon vegetable oil

2 tablespoons herb vinegar

salt and freshly ground black pepper

¼ teaspoon ground sweet paprika

serves 4

preparation + cooling 40 minutes

cooking 10 minutes

----

per serving 485 calories, 17g fat, 8g saturated fat, 63g carbohydrate, 7g sugar, 5g fibre, 2.4g salt

1 Cook pasta in plenty of lightly salted boiling water until *al dente*, following packet instructions. Drain, rinse under cold running water and leave to cool.

2 Place beans, 3 sprigs thyme and ½ teaspoon salt in a saucepan and cover with water. Cook, covered, 10 minutes or until crisp-tender. Drain, reserving cooking water. Briefly immerse in iced water and drain again.

3 Trim ham of excess fat and cut into narrow strips. Combine pasta, beans, shallots and ham in a large bowl. Finely chop leaves from remaining 3 sprigs thyme.

4 To make dressing, mix soured cream, 2 tablespoons cooking water, oil, vinegar, salt, pepper, sweet paprika and chopped thyme in a bowl until creamy.

5 Stir dressing into salad. Divide salad among serving bowls and garnish with radishes.

cook's tip

Don't overcook beans or they will lose their crunch and valuable nutrients. Plunge them into iced water immediately after cooking to stop the cooking process and help them retain their fresh, bright appearance.

Tortellini, carrot and egg salad

Here ricotta and spinach tortellini is used, but you could use another variety such as mushroom for a completely different flavour combination. Carrots that have been scored into flower shapes add fun to the presentation.

300g carrots

1 tablespoon vegetable oil

1 small onion, finely chopped

125ml vegetable stock

500g fresh tortellini filled with spinach and ricotta

1 small head butterhead lettuce

2 medium eggs, hard–boiled

herb cream

125g double cream

125g low–fat yoghurt

2 tablespoons lemon juice

½ teaspoon herb mustard

3 tablespoons fresh dill, chopped

3 tablespoons fresh parsley, chopped

salt and freshly ground black pepper

serves 4

preparation + cooling 30 minutes

cooking 10 minutes

----

per serving 571 calories, 28g fat, 14g saturated fat, 59g carbohydrate, 10g sugar, 2.5g fibre, 1.7g salt

1 Score five narrow grooves lengthways along each carrot, Slice carrots into thin rounds to create flower-shaped discs.

2 Heat oil in a nonstick pan and cook onion over medium heat until transparent. Add carrots and stock. Cover pan and cook about 5 minutes; carrots should be crisp-tender. Remove pan from heat. Leave to cool. Cook pasta in plenty of lightly salted boiling water until *al dente*, about 4 minutes. Drain, rinse under cold running water. Leave to cool.

3 To make herb cream, whisk cream, yoghurt, lemon juice and mustard in a large bowl until combined. Stir in herbs. Season with salt and pepper to taste.

4 Mix carrots and pasta into herb cream. Tear lettuce into large pieces and distribute among serving plates. Top with salad. Cut eggs into quarters and place on top.

eggs

Store eggs in the fridge because they will age more in a day at room temperature than in a week in a fridge.

Soba noodle salad

Garlic, ginger, soy sauce and peanut oil give an oriental feel to this warm noodle salad. Vary the chicken with tofu and a vegetable stock for a meat-free alternative.

185ml chicken stock

2 cloves garlic, crushed

½ teaspoon ground ginger

¼ teaspoon dried crushed chilli

350g skinless chicken breast fillets

300g soba (buckwheat) noodles

250g green beans, cut in halves

2 medium carrots (about 250g),
   cut into matchsticks

1 tablespoon soft brown sugar

1 tablespoon salt–reduced soy sauce

1 tablespoon peanut or vegetable oil

175g finely shredded green cabbage

serves 4

preparation 20 minutes

cooking 15 minutes

per serving 300 calories, 6g fat, 1g saturated fat, 36g carbohydrate, 12g sugar, 4g fibre, 0.8g salt

1 Combine stock, garlic, ginger and chilli in a large pan; bring to a boil. Reduce heat to a simmer. Add chicken and cook, covered, 10 minutes, or until cooked through, turning once. Transfer chicken to a plate, reserving cooking liquid. Slice chicken thinly when cool.

2 Cook noodles in plenty of boiling water until *al dente*, according to packet instructions. Add beans and carrots for final minute of cooking time; drain.

3 Whisk brown sugar, soy sauce, oil and reserved cooking liquid in a large bowl. Add chicken, noodles, beans, carrots and cabbage; mix thoroughly. Serve at room temperature.

buckwheat

Buckwheat, from which soba noodles and kasha (roasted buckwheat) are made, is not a true grain; actually it's the fruit of a rhubarb-like plant. It contains more lysine, an essential amino acid, than grains and is gluten-free.

Noodle and squid salad

You can buy squid both fresh and frozen. Cook it for the shortest possible time to stop it from becoming rubbery. Red chillies and a dash of ginger, along with vermicelli noodles give the dish Far Eastern heat.

3 red chillies, seeded and finely chopped

pinch of salt

1 teaspoon freshly ground black pepper

500g cleaned small squid or calamari, halved

1 tablespoon vegetable oil

100g rice vermicelli

1 small red onion, finely sliced

2 teaspoons fresh ginger, grated

2 teaspoons Asian fish sauce

3 tablespoons soy sauce

2 tablespoons lime juice

3 tablespoons fresh coriander, chopped

2 teaspoons soft brown sugar

serves 4

preparation + soaking 10 minutes

cooking 1 minute

1 Combine chillies, salt and pepper in a medium bowl. Brush squid with oil. Add to bowl and toss to coat with chillies.

2 Pour boiling water over vermicelli; leave 5 minutes or until softened. Drain.

3 Toss vermicelli, onion, ginger, fish sauce, soy sauce, lime juice, coriander and sugar in a serving bowl.

4 Heat a ridged grill pan or heavy-based frying pan. Add squid, cook over high heat about 30 seconds on each side. Serve on top of noodles.

per serving 240 calories, 5g fat, 1g saturated fat. 28g carbohydrate, 6g sugar, 0.5g fibre, 2.3g salt

Noodle and mushroom sweet and sour salad

A symbol of longevity in Asia where they are considered to have significant health-promoting properties, shiitake mushrooms have a rich, smoky taste and a meaty texture.

250g cellophane noodles

250g fresh shiitake mushrooms

250g Chinese cabbage

2 medium carrots (about 250g)

3 tablespoons vegetable oil

1 clove garlic, finely chopped

1 tablespoon fresh ginger root,
   finely chopped

2 tablespoons soy sauce

2 tablespoons rice vinegar

2 teaspoons soft brown sugar

1 tablespoon lime juice

salt and freshly ground black pepper

2 red chillies, finely sliced

serves 4

preparation + soaking 30 minutes

cooking 10 minutes

----

per serving 351 calories, 9g fat, 1g saturated fat, 60g carbohydrate, 8g sugar, 3g fibre, 1.4g salt

1 Pour boiling water over noodles; leave 10 minutes. Wipe mushrooms with kitchen paper, remove stalks and slice large caps in half, leaving others whole.

2 Slice cabbage into quarters and remove core. Slice cabbage thinly. Cut carrots into fine strips. Drain noodles and cut into short lengths.

3 Combine noodles, cabbage and carrots in a bowl. Heat oil in a pan and sauté mushrooms over high heat. Add garlic and ginger and cook another 3 minutes. Stir in soy sauce and 1 tablespoon rice vinegar. Remove from heat. Add brown sugar, lime juice and salt and pepper to taste. Leave to cool.

4 Combine mushroom mixture and noodle mixture. Add remaining 1 tablespoon rice vinegar and season to taste with salt and pepper. Distribute among individual serving dishes. Sprinkle with chillies.

cook's tip

Cellophane noodles must not be boiled. Soak them in hot water and wait until they are soft before cutting them into shorter sections with kitchen scissors. Cellophane noodles (also known as glass noodles) are available from Asian supermarkets and many online suppliers.

Salami rice salad

Many rice salads are relatively dry in texture, but this one is a complete contrast. A yoghurt and mayonnaise dressing binds spicy sausage with steamed broccoli and yellow peppers in a satisfying main course salad.

140g long-grain rice

350ml vegetable stock

500g broccoli

1 medium yellow pepper

250g spicy salami, in one piece

leaves of 3 sprigs thyme, finely chopped

½ teaspoon ground sweet paprika

dressing

3 tablespoons light mayonnaise

125g yoghurt

1 tablespoon olive oil

2 tablespoons white wine vinegar

herb salt

freshly ground black pepper

serves 4

preparation + cooling 30 minutes

cooking 35 minutes

----

per serving 540 calories, 33g fat, 11g saturated fat, 36g carbohydrate, 8g sugar, 4g fibre, 3.3g salt

1 Place rice and stock in a saucepan, cover and bring to a boil. Reduce heat to low, half cover pan and cook rice 15 to 20 minutes or until cooked. Remove from heat. Let stand, uncovered, until cool, loosening rice occasionally with a fork.

2 Chop broccoli into small pieces. Place in a steamer basket. Fill a large saucepan with water to a depth equal to the width of two fingers; bring to a boil. Reduce heat to a simmer. Place steamer basket on top of pan. Cover; cook broccoli 8 to 12 minutes, or until crisp-tender. Remove from steamer and leave to cool. Reserve cooking liquid.

3 Halve pepper and cut into small strips. Peel salami and cut into small strips.

4 To make dressing, whisk mayonnaise, yoghurt, oil and 1 tablespoon vinegar in a large bowl until well combined. Add herb salt and pepper to taste. Add rice, vegetables and salami and stir to combine. If salad is too dry, mix in 3 to 4 tablespoons of reserved cooking liquid.

5 Mix half the thyme into the salad. Check seasoning, adding remaining 1 tablespoon vinegar and salt and pepper to taste. Sprinkle with paprika and remaining thyme.

cook's tip

Chorizo, a Spanish sausage made from coarsely chopped fatty pork seasoned with smoked paprika, may be used in this recipe instead of salami. Fry slices until crisp over a high heat and drain off fat before using.

Spicy brown rice salad with feta

Mix nutty brown rice with aubergines and garlic and add a helping of ajvar, an aubergine and pepper relish. Feta, olives and baby aubergines finish it off perfectly.

200g brown rice

½ teaspoon salt

300g mini or large aubergines

5 tablespoons olive oil

1 clove garlic, finely sliced

2 tablespoons ajvar (spicy pepper and aubergine relish; see below)

3 tablespoons lemon juice

½ to 1 teaspoon dried chilli flakes

finely chopped leaves of 4 sprigs mint

salt and freshly ground black pepper

3 large tomatoes, diced

heart of 1 cos lettuce

125g feta cheese, cubed

100g kalamata olives

serves **4**

preparation **30 minutes (overnight soaking)**

cooking **1 hour**

per serving 445 calories, 26g fat, 7g saturated fat, 46g carbohydrate, 5g sugar, 4g fibre, 2.4g salt

1 Mix rice, 500ml water and ½ teaspoon salt in a saucepan. Cover and soak overnight. Bring rice to a boil, uncovered. Cook half covered over low heat for 40 minutes. Remove from heat; leave to cool. Loosen rice occasionally with a fork.

2 Leave mini aubergines whole. Dice large ones. Heat 3 tablespoons oil in a nonstick pan over medium heat. Cook aubergines about 10 minutes, turning occasionally.

3 Add garlic and cook 2 minutes. Remove pan from heat, leave to cool.

4 Combine ajvar, 2 tablespoons lemon juice, remaining 2 tablespoons oil, chilli flakes and mint in a large bowl; season with salt and pepper to taste. Mix in cooked rice and tomatoes. Season with remaining 1 tablespoon lemon juice and salt and pepper to taste.

5 Line a serving plate with lettuce. Top with salad, aubergines, feta and olives.

Spicy pepper and aubergine relish

Ajvar is a spiced aubergine and pepper relish that's a favourite in the Balkan region. You should be able to get it at a shop that stocks European specialities. Or make your own.

✳ Heat **75ml olive oil** in a large frying pan. Fry **2 large chopped onions** until soft and golden. Add **4 large diced aubergines, 4 chopped garlic cloves** and **1 bay leaf** and stir until aubergine has softened.

✳ Add **200ml white wine, 3 sun-dried tomatoes, chopped finely** and **juice of 3 lemons**. Season and cover. Simmer for 8-10 minutes, stirring frequently. Remove lid and cook for 2–3 minutes, adding a little extra wine if needed.

✳ Heat grill and place **3 large red peppers, halved, cored and quartered** on a baking tray, skin side up. Grill until skins are blackened. When cool, peel off skins and chop peppers. Remove aubergine mixture from heat and cool slightly. Stir in **75ml olive oil** and the red peppers. Season to taste.

Spicy brown rice salad with feta

Paella with chicken and prawns

In Spain, paellas are rustled up in huge dishes over a fire on the beach. This is a salad version: the rice and vegetables are left to cool; chicken and prawns are marinated for a few minutes then cooked.

3 tablespoons olive oil

200g risotto (arborio) rice

¼ teaspoon ground saffron

3 tablespoons dry white wine

500ml chicken stock

1 bay leaf

120g frozen green peas

100g frozen green beans

3 tablespoons lemon juice

2 tablespoons sherry vinegar

salt and freshly ground black pepper

1 medium red pepper

2 medium tomatoes

heart of 1 cos lettuce

chicken and prawns

250g skinless chicken breast fillets

12 medium–size uncooked prawns

2 cloves garlic, thinly sliced

2 tablespoons lemon juice

1 tablespoon olive oil

salt and freshly ground black pepper

3 tablespoons olive oil (for frying)

lemon wedges, for garnish

serves **4**

preparation + standing **1 hour 30 minutes**

cooking **20 minutes**

- -

per serving 520 calories, 22g fat, 3.5g saturated fat, 49g carbohydrate, 6g sugar, 3.5g fibre, 0.8g salt

1 Heat 1 ½ tablespoons oil in a saucepan. Add rice and saffron and cook, stirring, until transparent. Add wine, stock, 4 tablespoons water and bay leaf. Bring to a boil. Add peas and beans and cook until rice has absorbed all the liquid. Remove from heat.

2 Combine rice, peas and beans in a large bowl. Whisk remaining 1 ½ tablespoons oil, lemon juice and vinegar until combined. Add salt and pepper to taste. Stir into rice mixture. Leave 1 hour in a cool place.

3 Chop pepper in half and cut into dice. Pour boiling water over tomatoes, leave 2 minutes then plunge into iced water. Peel and dice. Mix pepper and tomatoes into rice.

4 Cut chicken into thin strips and place in a bowl with half the garlic and 1 tablespoon lemon juice. Peel and clean prawns (see right). Place in a bowl with remaining garlic, remaining 1 tablespoon lemon juice, 1 tablespoon olive oil, salt and pepper.

5 Heat 3 tablespoons oil in a heavy pan over high heat. Add chicken mixture; sear chicken quickly on all sides. Add prawn mixture and sear prawns on both sides. Reduce heat to medium. Cook another 5 minutes or until done. Arrange lettuce leaves on a large platter. Top with rice salad and chicken and prawn mixture. Garnish with lemon wedges.

cook's tip

Arborio rice is a creamy textured, medium–grain Italian rice that is used in making paella and risotto because it remains firm in the centre. It absorbs a large amount of stock during cooking.

peeling prawns

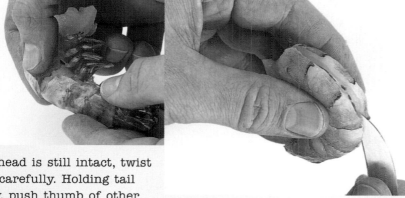

1 If head is still intact, twist it off carefully. Holding tail firmly, push thumb of other hand through shell and remove.

2 Cut along back of prawn with a small, sharp knife. Pull out black intestinal tract with fingertips or a knife. Discard.

3 Rinse prawns under cold running water. Place on kitchen paper and pat dry.

Rice salad with ginger-soy dressing

The Hindi word *basmati* means fragrant. It refers to the nut-like flavour and aroma of this small but long-grained rice. It makes a great base for a Chinese-inspired salad with cashews, bamboo shoots and a ginger dressing.

140g basmati or other fragrant rice

½ teaspoon salt

125g fresh baby sweetcorn (about 10)

150g mangetout

1 medium red pepper

3 spring onions, finely chopped

1 can (190g) bamboo shoots, drained

4 tablespoons roasted cashew nuts

ginger–soy dressing

1 tablespoon fresh ginger root, finely grated

3 tablespoons rice vinegar

2 tablespoons soy sauce

2 tablespoons sunflower or peanut oil

1 tablespoon medium–hot mango chutney

serves 4

preparation + cooling 1 hour

cooking 20 to 25 minutes

---

per serving 318 calories, 14g fat, 2.5g saturated fat, 39g carbohydrate, 8g sugar, 3g fibre, 2.1g salt

1 Combine rice, 250ml water and salt in a saucepan and bring to a boil. Half cover rice and cook over low heat 20 to 25 minutes. Remove from heat. Leave to cool. Loosen rice occasionally with a fork.

2 Bring a pan of lightly salted water to a boil. Blanch sweetcorn 3 minutes and mangetout 1 minute. Drain, immerse in iced water to arrest cooking. Drain; leave to cool.

3 Halve pepper and cut into narrow strips. Cut mangetout and sweetcorn in half. Mix rice and all the salad vegetables in a large bowl.

4 To make ginger-soy dressing, combine vinegar, soy sauce, oil and chutney in a bowl. (If chutney has large pieces of mango, break up with a fork before adding.) Stir to combine.

5 Stir dressing into rice salad. Arrange salad on serving plates and sprinkle with cashew nuts.

cook's tip

Rice is classified by size and shape (long, medium and short grain). Long–grain rice remains separate and dry when cooked and is ideal for use in rice salads.

Spicy rice salad with pineapple

A sweet and sour salad that puts together crunchy celery, mushrooms and pineapple with basmati rice is topped with a creamy curry vinaigrette.

185g basmati rice

½ teaspoon salt

200g canned pineapple slices or pieces in natural juice, drained

4 stalks celery

300g small mushrooms, chopped

2 spring onions, sliced

4 to 6 large Chinese cabbage leaves

curry vinaigrette

100g crème fraîche or soured cream

3 tablespoons milk

2 tablespoons raspberry vinegar

1 tablespoon sunflower oil

¼ teaspoon ground ginger

1 teaspoon mild curry powder

¼ to ½ teaspoon sambal oelek or Chinese chilli paste

serves 4

preparation + cooling 40 minutes

cooking 25 minutes

per serving 336 calories, 14g fat, 7.5g saturated fat, 46g carbohydrate, 8g sugar, 2g fibre, 0.6g salt

1 Place rice in a saucepan with 400ml water and ½ teaspoon salt. Bring to a boil, uncovered. Cover pan and cook rice over low heat 15 to 20 minutes or until all liquid is absorbed. Rice should be light and fluffy with steam holes on the surface. Turn off heat, let stand, covered, another 5 minutes. Remove from heat, uncover pan and let rice cool. Loosen grains occasionally with a fork.

2 Chop pineapple slices into small pieces. Slice celery into thin strips. Reserve feathery leaves. Combine rice, pineapple, celery and mushrooms in a large bowl. Add spring onions, reserving a few for garnish.

3 To make dressing, whisk crème fraîche, milk, vinegar, oil, ginger, curry and ¼ teaspoon sambal oelek in a bowl until creamy. Add remaining ¼ teaspoon sambal oelek to taste. Stir into salad ingredients.

4 Cut Chinese cabbage leaves into strips. Divide among individual serving plates and top with rice salad. Garnish with celery leaves and reserved spring onion rings.

cook's tip

Basmati is an aromatic rice native to Pakistan and India. It is good for steaming or boiling. The grains swell lengthways only when cooked and stay separate and dry.

Wild rice salad with tomatoes and chillies

Wild rice is actually not a rice, but a tall aquatic grass that grows in Japan, China and the Great Lakes region of North America. Here it gets extra flavour from hot chillies, but mozzarella makes the whole dish more mellow.

1 tablespoon olive oil

1 medium onion, finely diced

105g wild rice

90g long–grain rice

400ml vegetable stock

8 pickled hot green chillies, drained

4 plum tomatoes, cored and thinly sliced

150g rocket

250g baby mozzarella balls

pesto vinaigrette

3 tablespoons olive oil

3 tablespoons red wine vinegar

2 tablespoons red (sun–dried tomato) pesto

salt and freshly ground black pepper

serves 4

preparation + chilling 1 hour

cooking 30 minutes

per serving 526 calories, 29g fat, 11g saturated fat, 46g carbohydrate, 5g sugar, 2g fibre, 1.1g salt

1 Heat oil in a saucepan and sauté onion until transparent. Stir in wild rice and long-grain rice. Add stock and bring to a boil, uncovered. Cover pan; cook over low heat 15 to 20 minutes or until all liquid is absorbed. The rice should be light and fluffy with steam holes on the surface. Turn off heat, let stand, covered, 5 minutes. Remove pan from heat, uncover and let cool. Loosen grains occasionally with a fork.

2 Remove seeds from 4 chillies; slice into rounds. Keep remaining chillies whole.

3 To make pesto vinaigrette, whisk oil, vinegar, pesto, salt and pepper in a large bowl. Carefully fold in cooked rice, chopped chillies and tomatoes.

4 Divide rocket leaves among plates. Spoon rice salad onto plates. Add mozzarella. Garnish with whole chillies.

health guide

Wild rice contains more protein than rice and is richer in lysine, the amino acid that is lacking in most grains. Amino acids are essential for human growth and function.

Wild rice salad with tomatoes and chillies

Wild rice salad with shallots and lettuce

✳ Prepare **rice mixture** as described in the main recipe, omitting the onion; let cool.
Heat **2 tablespoons olive oil** in a nonstick pan, add **300g whole peeled shallots** and **125ml dry
red wine**. Cook, covered, 10 minutes. Uncover, and cook until wine has almost evaporated.

✳ Stir in **2 tablespoons balsamic vinegar**, **2 tablespoons olive oil**, **1 teaspoon chopped fresh
rosemary leaves** and **salt** and **pepper** to taste. Let cool. Stir in rice. Line a platter with
cos lettuce leaves. Top with rice salad.

Warm lentil salad

The flavours from the thyme, spring onions and vinegar dressing will deepen over time so the salad may be even more delicious the following day.

200g brown lentils

1 medium carrot, diced

2 teaspoons fresh thyme leaves

salt and freshly ground black pepper

6 plum tomatoes, chopped

2 spring onions, finely sliced

3 teaspoons olive oil

2 tablespoons red wine vinegar

2 teaspoons Dijon mustard

serves 4

preparation 10 minutes

cooking 30 minutes

per serving 209 calories, 5g fat, 1g saturated fat, 31g carbohydrate, 7g sugar, 6.5g fibre, 0.3g salte

1 Place lentils, carrot, thyme and salt and pepper in a large saucepan; cover with water. Bring to a boil. Cover pan; cook, simmering, 25 minutes or until lentils are tender. Drain.

2 Place lentil mixture in a serving bowl with tomatoes and spring onions. Whisk oil, vinegar and mustard and stir in.

health guide

Lentils and other legumes are a good source of copper, a trace mineral that may help lower blood cholesterol. The iron content of lentils is more easily absorbed by the body if they are cooked or served with a food that is rich in vitamin C, such as tomatoes or cabbage.

Potato and lentil salad

Lentils and potatoes give substance, while salty olives, capers and spring onions dressed with lemon and wine vinegar, add extra taste.

1kg waxy potatoes, peeled and
    cut into large chunks

125ml olive oil

2 tablespoons red wine vinegar

750g cooked brown lentils

120g pitted black olives

1 tablespoon capers, chopped

2 cloves garlic, chopped

1 tablespoon lemon juice

55g flat-leaved parsley, roughly chopped

6 spring onions, sliced diagonally

freshly ground black pepper

serves 6
preparation 15 minutes
cooking 20 minutes

----

per serving 430 calories, 20g fat, 3g saturated fat,
51g carbohydrate, 2.5g sugar, 7.5g fibre, 0.8g salt

1 Cook potatoes in a pan of boiling water 20 minutes or until tender. Drain and transfer to a large bowl.

2 While potatoes are still hot, whisk oil and vinegar and stir in. Carefully mix in lentils, olives, capers, garlic, lemon juice, parsley, spring onions and a good grinding of pepper. Serve while still warm.

cook's tip

Dry salt-cured olives and those pickled in brine are high in sodium. Because capers are also salty, this salad needs no additional salt.

Lentil salad with fried onions and rosemary

Crispy rings of caramelised onion are a tasty addition to Puy lentils cooked with rosemary and bay and combined with potato and tomato.

400g Puy–style green lentils

1 small sprig rosemary

1 small dried bay leaf

3 small unpeeled cooked potatoes

2 large tomatoes, cored and diced

2 tablespoons olive oil

2 tablespoons red wine or herb vinegar

1 tablespoon lemon juice

1 teaspoon lemon peel, grated

½ teaspoon ground cumin

1 clove garlic, crushed

salt and freshly ground black pepper

2 large onions, sliced into rings

2 tablespoons olive oil

40g fresh flat–leaved parsley, finely chopped

serves 4

preparation + chilling 1 hour 35 minutes

cooking 40 minutes to 1 hour

-----

per serving 481 calories, 13g fat, 2g saturated fat, 67g carbohydrate, 7g sugar, 11g fibre, 0.1g salt

1 Place lentils, rosemary and bay leaf in a saucepan. Add water to cover; bring to a boil. Cook on medium heat about 40 minutes or until soft. Leave to cool in cooking liquid. Drain, reserving liquid. Discard rosemary and bay leaf.

2 Peel and dice potatoes and place in a large bowl with tomatoes and lentils. Whisk oil, vinegar, lemon juice, peel, cumin, garlic and 3 tablespoons reserved cooking liquid in a small bowl. Add salt and pepper to taste. Stir into salad. Chill salad, covered, 1 hour.

3 Cook onion rings in oil over moderate heat until golden brown. Check salad for seasoning, adding more salt, pepper and vinegar, if needed. Stir in parsley.

4 Distribute salad among individual serving bowls and top with warm onions.

Curried lentil salad

* Cook **lentils** as for main recipe and place in a serving bowl. Combine **1 tablespoon mild curry paste, 2 tablespoons mango chutney, 3 tablespoons olive oil, 2 tablespoons lime juice, 2 finely diced spring onions** and **1 teaspoon finely chopped fresh ginger**. Stir into lentils. Chill 1 hour.

* Grate **2 carrots**. Wash **250g baby spinach leaves**; cook briefly in the water clinging to the leaves. Add carrots and spinach to bowl. Add **salt** and **pepper** to taste and toss to combine. Serve with **pita bread**.

Lentil salad with fried onions and rosemary

White bean salad with sesame dressing

White bean salad with sesame dressing

Sesame paste or tahini is a staple of North African and Middle Eastern cookery. Here it gives an unusual flavour to white beans with mild green chillies, olives and red onion.

200g dried small white beans

2 medium tomatoes, cored and diced

1 medium red onion, thinly sliced

2 mild light green banana chillies,
   cut in thin strips

4 tablespoons olive oil

4 tablespoons red wine vinegar

salt and freshly ground black pepper

4 tablespoons tahini (sesame paste)

2 tablespoons lemon juice

2 medium eggs, hard–boiled, quartered

50g black olives

40g fresh parsley leaves

serves 4

preparation 25 minutes + 12 hours soaking

cooking 45 minutes

per serving 420 calories, 26g fat, 4g saturated fat,
30g carbohydrate, 5g sugar, 11g fibre, 0.5g salt

1 Soak beans in water overnight. Drain. Place in a pan and cover with water. Bring to a boil; cook 35 minutes or until soft. Let cool in cooking water. Drain.

2 Place beans in a serving bowl. Add tomatoes, onion and chillies. Whisk oil, vinegar, salt and pepper and stir into salad.

3 Combine tahini, lemon juice and about 4 tablespoons water in a bowl; stir until smooth. Add salt to taste. Add eggs, olives and parsley to salad. Spoon on sesame dressing.

health guide

Sesame seeds are a good source of calcium, magnesium, iron and zinc. They also contain two unique substances called sesamin and sesamolin, both of which have been shown to have a cholesterol-lowering effect in humans.

White bean salad with herb dressing

* Cook **250g dried small white beans** as for main recipe. Finely slice **3 spring onions**. Dice **2 small cucumbers**. Halve and dice **1 yellow pepper**. Combine all ingredients in a serving bowl.

* To make herb dressing, combine **125g soured cream** and **2 tablespoons olive oil**. Add **1 tablespoon finely chopped fresh marjoram**, **1 tablespoon finely chopped fresh mint leaves** and **1 tablespoon finely chopped fresh parsley**. Season generously with **salt and black pepper**.

* Pour dressing over salad and stir in. Serve with **toasted focaccia**.

Buckwheat and artichoke salad with feta

Buckwheat is not a grain or a type of wheat but is used as if it were. The hulled roasted seeds are called groats or kasha. When cooked, they have a nutty taste.

500ml vegetable stock

1 bay leaf

180g wholegrain roasted
   buckwheat groats (kasha)

2 teaspoons olive oil

1 can (280g) artichoke hearts, drained

1 medium head round radicchio

2 large tomatoes

1 sprig rosemary

4 sprigs marjoram

4 tablespoons olive oil

1 tablespoon balsamic vinegar

3 tablespoons lemon juice

salt and freshly ground black pepper

150g feta cheese, cubed

serves 4

preparation + cooling 1 hour 30 minutes

cooking 20 to 30 minutes

- -

per serving 410 calories, 21g fat, 7g saturated fat,
46g carbohydrate, 5g sugar, 4g fibre, 1.5g salt

1 Place stock, bay leaf and buckwheat in a saucepan and bring to a boil, uncovered. Add oil. Reduce heat to very low. Cover pan; simmer 15 minutes. Remove from heat and leave, covered, 10 minutes. Uncover; fluff buckwheat with a fork. Season with salt to taste. Let cool.

2 Chop artichoke hearts into small pieces. Tear radicchio into small pieces. Halve and core tomatoes, remove seeds. Cut flesh into small cubes.

3 Finely chop rosemary and marjoram leaves. Whisk herbs, oil, vinegar and 2 tablespoons lemon juice in a large serving bowl. Add salt and pepper to taste. Add buckwheat, artichokes, radicchio and tomatoes; stir to combine.

4 Leave salad, covered, 1 hour. Just before serving, add salt, pepper and remaining lemon juice to taste. Add feta and stir to combine.

health guide

Buckwheat contains rutin, which is a known cancer fighter. Rutin also helps to strengthen blood vessels, lower cholesterol levels and lower blood pressure.

Buckwheat and artichoke salad with feta

Roasted buckwheat salad with yoghurt dressing

✳ Prepare **180g wholegrain roasted buckwheat groats (kasha)** as for main recipe; let cool. Dice **2 large tomatoes** and **1** red and **1** green pepper. Slice **3 spring onions** into rings. Place all ingredients in a serving bowl.

✳ To make yoghurt dressing, mash **100g feta** in a bowl with **175g yoghurt**. Whisk in **2 tablespoons olive oil**, **2 tablespoons lemon juice** and **1 tablespoon white wine vinegar**. Add **salt** and **pepper** to taste. Stir into salad. Sprinkle with **2 tablespoons chopped fresh parsley**.

Couscous salad with chickpeas

Couscous salad with chickpeas

Couscous is an excellent base for a host of salad ingredients as it adds texture but allows the taste to come through. Little chunks of garlicky sausage and spring onions contrast with the milder chickpeas.

240g instant couscous

½ teaspoon salt

4 plum tomatoes

2 spring onions

40g fresh flat-leaved parsley, finely chopped

1 can (300g) chickpeas, rinsed and drained

200g garlic sausage in one piece

vinaigrette

4 tablespoons olive oil

1 tablespoon red wine vinegar

3 tablespoons lemon juice

1 clove garlic, crushed

1 teaspoon ground cumin

1 teaspoon ground sweet paprika

salt and freshly ground black pepper

serves 4

preparation + standing 35 minutes

per serving 453 calories, 22g fat, 5g saturated fat, 45g carbohydrate, 4g sugar, 1g fibre, 1.7g salt

1 Bring 250ml water to a boil in a medium saucepan. Remove from heat. Stir in couscous and salt and leave to absorb liquid 20 minutes. Leave to cool.

2 Halve and core tomatoes and cut into small dice. Slice spring onions into rings.

3 To make vinaigrette, whisk oil, vinegar, 2 tablespoons lemon juice, garlic, cumin and paprika in a large bowl. Add salt and pepper to taste. Stir parsley, couscous, chickpeas, tomatoes and spring onions into vinaigrette.

4 Just before serving, taste salad and season with salt, pepper and remaining 1 tablespoon lemon juice. Slice sausage into small cubes and stir in.

Couscous salad with tuna

❋ Prepare **240g couscous** as in main recipe. Halve **2 green peppers** and cut into strips. Finely dice **1 red onion**. Cut **2 courgettes** into thin strips. Mix all ingredients in a bowl.

❋ Whisk **3 tablespoons olive oil**, **3 tablespoons lemon juice**, **1 clove garlic, crushed**, **½ teaspoon ground sweet paprika** and **salt and pepper** to taste. Stir into couscous salad. Add **1 tablespoon chopped fresh mint leaves**. Stir in **150g drained, canned, finely flaked tuna**.

Chickpea, spinach and aubergine salad

Chickpeas, with their nutty, earthy taste, are used in many Mediterranean and Middle Eastern dishes. In this delicious salad they pair superbly with lightly fried aubergine, slivers of red onion and crumbly feta cheese.

2 medium aubergines (about 500g in total), thinly sliced

80ml olive oil

150g baby spinach leaves

175g cooked chickpeas

250g feta cheese, crumbled

1 small red onion, thinly sliced

3 tablespoons fresh mint leaves, chopped

2 tablespoons lemon juice

serves 4

preparation 5 minutes

cooking 6 minutes

per serving 374 calories, 28g fat, 11g saturated fat, 13g carbohydrate, 5g sugar, 3.5g fibre, 2.4g salt

1 Brush aubergine slices with half the oil. Place in a large nonstick pan over medium-high heat. Cook 2 to 3 minutes each side until golden.

2 Place spinach on a serving platter and top with aubergine, chickpeas, feta, onion and mint.

3 Combine remaining oil and lemon juice. Pour over salad. Serve at room temperature.

aubergine

Aubergines with the best flavour are of medium size with thin skins. Larger ones are more likely to be full of seeds and taste bitter. Bitter aubergines may be sprinkled with salt to draw out the flavour. Wash and pat dry before using.

Quinoa, avocado and chorizo salad

Quinoa, tomato juice and kidney beans are cooked together with red wine vinegar, lime juice and cumin and chilled. Thin slices of spicy chorizo sausage are then briefly fried and served warm on the cool base with cubes of avocado.

180g quinoa

500ml tomato juice

½ teaspoon salt

1 medium firm avocado

2 tablespoons lemon juice

1 medium red pepper, halved and finely diced

1 medium red onion, finely diced

250g canned kidney beans, drained and rinsed

150g chorizo, in one piece

vinaigrette

3 tablespoons olive oil

2 tablespoons red wine vinegar

1 to 2 tablespoons lime juice

½ teaspoon ground cumin

1 clove garlic, crushed

salt and freshly ground black pepper

serves 4

preparation + chilling 1 hour 30 minutes

cooking 20 minutes

per serving 490 calories, 27g fat, 7g saturated fat, 45g carbohydrate, 13g sugar, 6.5g fibre, 2.4g salt

1 Place quinoa, tomato juice and salt in a saucepan. Bring to a boil, uncovered. Cover pan and cook 10 to 15 minutes over low heat. Turn off heat, let stand, covered, 5 minutes. Remove from heat, uncover pan and let cool, occasionally loosening grains with a fork.

2 Dice avocado, place in a bowl and sprinkle with lemon juice to prevent discolouration. Place on a large serving plate with pepper, onion and kidney beans.

3 To make vinaigrette, whisk oil, vinegar, 1 tablespoon lime juice, ground cumin and garlic in a bowl. Add salt, pepper and remaining 1 tablespoon lime juice to taste.

4 Pour vinaigrette over salad and stir in. Chill salad, covered, 1 hour.

5 Peel chorizo and slice thinly. Heat a nonstick pan over medium heat and fry sausage on both sides until light golden. Drain and add to salad. Serve at once.

quinoa

Quinoa is often classified as a grain but actually comes from the same plant family as spinach. While the tops of the plant are edible, it is the seeds that are generally served. Quick cooking brings out the delicate flavour and makes the seeds fluffy. Quinoa is high in iron and protein and can be used as a substitute for rice.

Quinoa, avocado and chorizo salad

Quinoa with sweet and spicy dressing

✳ Prepare **180g quinoa** as in main recipe, using water in place of tomato juice. Place in a serving bowl.

✳ Thinly slice **3 red onions** and **300g baby carrots**. In a nonstick pan, heat **2 tablespoons peanut oil** over medium heat. Add carrots and cook 3 minutes. Add onions; cook 5 minutes. Add **100g baby spinach leaves**. Cook just until wilted. Transfer to serving bowl.

✳ To make dressing, whisk **4 tablespoons dry white wine, 2 tablespoons honey, ½ teaspoon sambal oelek (Indonesian chilli paste)** and **1 teaspoon mustard**. Stir into salad.

Meat & Poultry Salads

Marinades made with oils, vinegars and fresh herbs and stir-fry sauces that combine spicy Asian flavours enhance the taste of meat and poultry adding an extra dimension to your salads. Lean meat and poultry provide high-quality protein that's essential for growth and cell repair as well as iron and B vitamins.

Beef salad in cucumber herb marinade

Made with a beef cut that's generally used for slow cooking in stews and casseroles, this salad takes a while to complete and needs to be made in advance. Once you've cooked the meat, it's all about adding taste with a long, slow marinade.

500g beef chuck steak

2 medium onions, roughly chopped

2 celery stalks, roughly chopped

2 medium carrots (about 250g), roughly chopped

1 bay leaf

3 teaspoons salt

1 tablespoon whole black peppercorns

1 clove

200g sweet and sour pickled cucumbers from a jar

2 medium white onions

1 teaspoon allspice

5 tablespoons liquid from pickle jar

2 tablespoons sunflower or groundnut oil

2 tablespoons white wine vinegar

1 tablespoon fresh dill, finely chopped

1 tablespoon fresh parsley, finely chopped

serves 4

preparation 35 minutes

cooking 2 hours

marinating 12 hours

- -

per serving 295 calories, 13g fat, 4g saturated fat, 14g carbohydrate, 11g sugar, 3.5g fibre, 4g salt

1 Trim beef of fat. Place beef, roughly chopped vegetables, bay leaf, 2 teaspoons salt, 1 teaspoon peppercorns and the clove in a saucepan. Cover with water; bring to a boil. Skim any fat from surface with a slotted spoon. Continue cooking, partly covered, over low heat 2 hours. Remove pan from heat. Leave meat to cool in cooking liquid.

2 Dice cucumbers and onions and place in a large bowl. Remove meat from pan. Reserve cooking liquid and discard vegetables. Cut meat into small cubes. Add to bowl with remaining peppercorns and allspice and mix well.

3 To make marinade, combine cucumber pickle liquid, oil, 1 tablespoon vinegar and remaining 1 teaspoon salt. Pour marinade over meat mixture. Top up with cooking liquid so that meat mixture is completely covered. Marinate, covered, in refrigerator 12 hours.

4 Remove from refrigerator 30 minutes before serving. Stir in a little of the herbs. Taste and add remaining tablespoon vinegar, if needed. Spoon salad into serving bowls using a slotted spoon. Sprinkle with remaining herbs.

cook's tip

This is a useful recipe to make ahead. It keeps well for 3 days in the refrigerator and the flavours intensify.

Beef salad in cucumber herb marinade

Beef and potato salad with horseradish dressing

✳ Cook **500g lean beef** as for the main recipe, without the carrots and celery. Add **2 chopped carrots** and **2 chopped celery stalks** in the last 10 minutes of cooking; carrots and celery should still be crunchy.

✳ Remove meat, carrots and celery from stock. Let cool; chop into small pieces. Place in a serving bowl. Dice **1 small red onion** and **4 medium cooked potatoes**. Add to bowl and mix well.

✳ To make horseradish dressing, whisk **200g light soured cream** with **2 tablespoons olive oil**, **2 tablespoons white wine vinegar** and **1 tablespoon horseradish cream**. Add **1 small apple, finely grated** and **salt** and **pepper** to taste. Add **2 tablespoons chopped fresh parsley**. Serve with meat salad.

Beef salad with lentils

Place slices of lightly-fried beef – here cooked rare, but adjust to your liking – on a bed of Puy lentils and chopped carrots and dress with horseradish cream.

1 tablespoon wholegrain mustard

6 tablespoons olive oil

generous pinch of ground black pepper

2 beef rump steaks (about 500g in total)

200g Puy–style green lentils

1 small sprig rosemary

300ml beef stock

2 medium carrots (about 250g), diced

½ teaspoon salt

freshly ground black pepper

3 tablespoons red wine vinegar

1 tablespoon fresh thyme leaves, chopped

4 tablespoons double cream

2 teaspoons horseradish cream

100g lamb's lettuce

3 tablespoons chives, finely chopped

serves 4

preparation 40 minutes

cooking 40 minutes

per serving 561 calories, 32g fat, 9g saturated fat, 31g carbohydrate, 6.5g sugar, 6.6g fibre, 2.3g salt

1 Combine mustard, 1 tablespoon oil and pepper. Rub steaks with mixture. Cover and chill until ready to cook. Place lentils, rosemary and stock in a pan. Bring to a boil, uncovered. Cover, cook lentils over low heat 20 minutes. Add carrots; cook another 10 minutes. Remove pan from heat. Leave lentils and carrots to cool in cooking liquid. Remove rosemary. Add ½ teaspoon salt.

2 Heat 1 tablespoon oil in a nonstick frying pan over medium-high heat. Add steaks; cook 3 to 5 minutes each side. Remove from pan, wrap in aluminium foil.

3 Whisk remaining 4 tablespoons oil and 2 tablespoons vinegar in a medium bowl. Add salt and pepper to taste. Drain lentils and carrots from pan and add to bowl. Stir in thyme. Whip cream in a small bowl until stiff; fold in the horseradish cream.

4 Slice steaks thinly and add any juices from meat to lentil mixture. Add remaining 1 tablespoon vinegar and salt and pepper to taste. Place lentil mixture on serving plates with lamb's lettuce. Add meat, top with a little horseradish cream mixture and sprinkle with chives. Serve remaining horseradish cream mixture separately.

Thai beef salad

Red chillies and lime, soy and garlic provide the Thai elements in
this super healthy beef salad served with lots of steamed broccoli.

500g beef rump steak

90ml salt–reduced soy sauce

2 cloves garlic, crushed

5 tablespoons lime juice

500g broccoli

20g fresh mint leaves

20g fresh basil leaves

15g fresh coriander leaves

1 small cucumber, halved lengthways
    and sliced

2 red chillies, thinly sliced

2 teaspoons soft brown sugar

serves 4

preparation 25 minutes

cooking 10 minutes

per serving 227 calories, 6g fat, 2.5g saturated fat,
13g carbohydrate, 12g sugar, 3.5g fibre, 3.5g salt

1 Place steak, 45ml soy sauce, garlic and 2 tablespoons
lime juice in a large bowl. Leave 10 minutes.

2 Heat grill to high heat; cook steak 2 minutes each side.
Set aside.

3 Place broccoli in a steamer basket. Fill a large pan with
boiling water to a depth equal to the width of two fingers;
bring to a boil. Reduce heat to a simmer. Place steamer
basket on top of pan. Cover, cook broccoli 5 to 6 minutes or
until crisp–tender. Leave to cool 10 minutes. Place in a large
bowl with mint, basil and coriander. Add cucumber slices.

4 Slice steak and add to salad. Combine chillies, sugar,
remaining 45ml soy sauce and remaining 3 tablespoons
lime juice in a bowl. Stir gently into salad. Pile salad onto
serving plates.

Mexican beef salad

This spicy salad combines strips of iron-rich beef with vitamin-packed vegetables, including baby sweetcorn, carrots, tomatoes and peppers. It makes a sustaining main meal.

500g cooked lean beef
2 long red chillies
30g fresh coriander leaves, finely chopped
4 tablespoons olive oil
3 tablespoons red wine vinegar
2 tablespoons lime juice
¼ teaspoon sweet ground paprika
salt and freshly ground black pepper
1 red and 1 orange pepper
8 canned baby sweetcorn spears,
    drained and rinsed
2 large tomatoes
2 spring onions, thinly sliced
50g tortilla chips

serves 4
preparation 35 minutes
marinating 1 hour

per serving 429 calories, 21g fat, 5g saturated fat, 17.5g carbohydrate, 7g sugar, 3g fibre, 0.5g salt

1 Cut beef into narrow strips; place in a bowl. Chop chillies finely; discard seeds. Add to bowl. Add coriander, reserving 1 tablespoon for garnish.

2 To make vinaigrette, whisk oil, 2 tablespoons vinegar, lime juice and paprika in a bowl. Add salt and pepper to taste. Stir into beef mixture. Chill, covered, 1 hour.

3 Dice peppers. Cut baby sweetcorn spears in half. Halve tomatoes, remove core and seeds; dice. Add to beef mixture with spring onions and remaining 1 tablespoon vinegar.

4 Just before serving, add salt and pepper to taste. Divide salad among serving bowls. Add tortilla chips and sprinkle with reserved coriander.

health guide

Beef is a leading source of high-quality protein and the vitamins B_{12} and B_6. It also contains such essential minerals as zinc and iron.

Pastrami and artichoke salad

Pastrami and artichoke salad

An American sandwich favourite, pastrami is strongly flavoured, but does not overwhelm the other ingredients, including delicate artichoke hearts, sweet plum tomatoes, red onion and rocket.

300g thinly sliced pastrami

4 tablespoons olive oil

1 tablespoon balsamic vinegar

2 tablespoons lemon juice

salt and freshly ground black pepper

100g rocket

6 artichoke hearts from a jar, drained

3 ripe plum tomatoes, sliced

1 medium red onion, thinly sliced into rings

serves 4

preparation + chilling 1 hour 35 minutes

per serving 238 calories, 15g fat, 3g saturated fat, 10g carbohydrate, 8g sugar, 2g fibre, 1.7g salt

1 Place pastrami on a plate. To make vinaigrette, whisk oil, vinegar and lemon juice in a bowl. Add salt and pepper to taste. Drizzle half the vinaigrette over pastrami. Chill, covered, 1 hour.

2 Line serving plates with rocket. Cut artichoke hearts into quarters and arrange on plates with tomatoes. Add pastrami and top with onion rings. Drizzle with remaining vinaigrette.

pastrami

Pastrami is made from highly seasoned beef. The meat is trimmed of fat and the surface then rubbed with salt and a combination of seasonings such as garlic, ground cinnamon, black pepper, paprika, cloves, coriander seeds and allspice. The meat is dry-cured, smoked and cooked. A Turkish version, known as pastirma, is also made from beef. This type is dried.

Pastrami salad on potatoes

✳ Marinate **300g sliced pastrami** as for the main recipe.

✳ Thinly slice **4 cooked, large potatoes**. Overlap slices on individual serving plates. Sprinkle with a little **ground cumin** and a little **ground paprika**. Add salt and **pepper** to taste. Drizzle on **2 tablespoons olive oil**.

✳ Slice **12 cherry tomatoes** in half; place on potatoes. Top with pastrami.

Spicy sausage and cheese salad

Most types of German-style sausages or wurst include pork, spices and peppercorns. In this salad, sausage and all the other ingredients, including Emmental cheese and strips of pickled gherkin are attractively sliced.

400g German-style cooked sausage or salami

250g reduced-fat Emmental cheese, thinly sliced

150g small gherkins in vinegar

2 medium red onions

30g chives, finely chopped

vinaigrette

2 tablespoons vegetable oil

3 to 4 tablespoons white wine vinegar

4 tablespoons gherkin liquid

4 tablespoons beef stock (broth)

1 teaspoon hot mustard

salt and freshly ground black pepper

serves 4

preparation 20 minutes

marinating 1 hour

per serving 566 calories, 43g fat, 17g saturated fat, 8g carbohydrate, 37g protein, 10g sugar, 3g fibre, 3g salt

1 Peel sausage and cut into fine strips. Cut cheese and gherkins into fine strips. Finely dice onions. Combine sausage, cheese, gherkins and onions in a large bowl.

2 To make vinaigrette, whisk oil, vinegar, 2 tablespoons gherkin liquid, stock and mustard in a bowl. Add salt and pepper to taste.

3 Pour vinaigrette over salad and toss to combine. Chill, covered, 1 hour. Add remaining 2 tablespoons gherkin liquid and salt and pepper to taste. Sprinkle with chives.

cook's tip

This salad has a sharp taste and a crunchy texture. Drained pickled cabbage (sauerkraut) may be used in place of the gherkins. Alternatively, you could use mixed pickled vegetables.

Veal and mushroom salad with basil

If you don't want to use veal, another light meat such as chicken or turkey would work well in this dish. The sauce is enhanced with a little port for a bit of luxury.

500g veal or chicken escalopes, cut thin

5 tablespoons olive oil

1 clove garlic, finely chopped

3 spring onions (scallions), finely sliced

500g mixed small mushrooms, such as button, Swiss brown or shiitake, sliced

salt and freshly ground black pepper

60g basil leaves

50g Parmesan, in one piece

4 tablespoons beef stock

2 tablespoons port wine

2 tablespoons balsamic vinegar

150g cherry tomatoes, cut in half

serves 4

preparation 15 minutes

cooking 15 minutes

per serving 360 calories, 21g fat, 5g saturated fat, 5g carbohydrate, 5g sugar, 2g fibre, 0.5g salt

1 Cut veal into thin, even strips. Heat 3 tablespoons oil in nonstick pan over high heat. Sear veal briefly on both sides. Add garlic and spring onions; cook 1 minute. Transfer to a plate and keep warm.

2 Heat remaining 2 tablespoons oil in pan. Fry mushrooms over medium heat 5 minutes. Add salt and pepper to taste. Transfer to a plate. Slice basil finely; keep a few leaves whole for garnish. Use a vegetable peeler to shave Parmesan into thin slices.

3 Place stock and port in pan in which veal was cooked; bring to a boil and cook briefly over high heat, stirring in juices and any crusty pieces from the meat. Transfer to a bowl. Add vinegar and salt and pepper to taste. When cooled completely, mix in two thirds of chopped basil.

4 Combine veal and mushrooms; place on a serving plate. Drizzle on stock mixture. Top with Parmesan. Garnish with remaining chopped basil, whole basil leaves and tomatoes.

Veal salad with beans

✻ Slice **500g green beans** into short lengths. Cook beans with **3 sprigs thyme** in lightly salted boiling water over medium heat 5 minutes. Drain; let cool. Discard thyme. Finely slice **3 spring onions**. Cut **8 cherry tomatoes** in half. Cut **500g veal escalopes** into thin strips. Heat **2 tablespoons vegetable oil** in nonstick pan. Cook veal over high heat 3 to 4 minutes. Season with **salt and pepper.**

✻ Whisk **2 tablespoons tarragon vinegar, 1 tablespoon white wine vinegar, 3 tablespoons vegetable oil** and a pinch of **sugar** in a large bowl. Add **salt** and **pepper** to taste. Add beans, onions, tomatoes and veal. Add salt and pepper to taste. Garnish with **1 tablespoon finely chopped fresh parsley.**

**Veal and mushroom salad
with basil**

Spicy pork salad

Cook the pork beforehand or use leftovers from a Sunday roast. Then cut into slim strips and mix together with Chinese cabbage, mangetout and an Eastern inspired dressing with a little Chinese chilli for extra zest.

500g cooked lean pork

250g Chinese cabbage

1 can (190g) bamboo shoots, drained

100g mangetout

1 small piece fresh ginger root

1 tablespoon lemongrass, chopped

2 tablespoons vegetable oil

½ teaspoon sesame oil

3 tablespoons rice vinegar

2 tablespoons salt–reduced soy sauce

1 teaspoon soft brown sugar

salt, to taste

2 tablespoons sesame seeds

2 tablespoons soured cream

1 teaspoon sambal oelek or
   Chinese chilli paste

3 tablespoons finely chopped chives

serves 4

preparation 30 minutes

per serving 371 calories, 21g fat, 6g saturated fat, 6g carbohydrate, 5.5g sugar, 2.5g fibre, 1g salt

1 Cut pork into very thin strips and place in a bowl. Finely shred Chinese cabbage. Cut bamboo shoots into thin strips. Cut mangetout into strips. Add all vegetables to bowl.

2 Finely chop ginger. Remove hard outer layers from lemongrass and finely chop tender part (see below).

3 To make vinaigrette, whisk vegetable oil, sesame oil, 2 tablespoons rice vinegar, soy sauce and sugar in a bowl. Add ginger and lemongrass; whisk to combine. Check seasoning, adding salt to taste. Stir vinaigrette into salad.

4 Toast sesame seeds in a frying pan over medium heat until golden, stirring occasionally. Transfer to a plate; set aside to cool. Combine soured cream and sambal oelek.

5 Taste salad, adding salt and remaining 1 tablespoon rice vinegar, if necessary. Spoon salad onto serving plates. Top with a little soured cream mixture. Sprinkle with sesame seeds and chives.

to prepare lemongrass

1 Remove outside woody layers from lemongrass and cut off root.

2 Trim woody ends from leaves. Wash lemongrass and pat dry with kitchen paper.

3 Cut tender leaves crossways in fine strips or chop finely. Or, grind them to a fine paste.

Mixed salad with ham

Smoked ham has a lots of flavour, but use a less salty variety if you prefer. The main ingredients will keep well for a day or so; add the bean sprouts or cress at the last minute so they don't get soggy.

250g smoked ham

200g frozen peas

salt

2 medium carrots (about 250g)

2 small cucumbers

100g pickled onions, drained

2 large tomatoes, cored and diced

100g lamb's lettuce

alfalfa or mung bean sprouts or
    cress, for garnish

creamy dressing

3 tablespoons mayonnaise

170g Greek-style yoghurt

1 teaspoon Dijon mustard

2 tablespoons lemon juice

pinch of sugar

salt and freshly ground black pepper

serves 4

preparation 25 minutes

cooking 5 minutes

----

per serving 288 calories, 16.5g fat, 5g saturated fat, 18g carbohydrate, 13g sugar, 6g fibre, 2g salt

1 Trim excess fat from ham; cut ham into small cubes. Cook peas in lightly salted boiling water for 5 minutes. Drain, reserving cooking liquid. Leave peas to cool.

2 Coarsely grate carrots. Quarter cucumbers lengthways, scoop out seeds with a small spoon and cut flesh into small pieces. Cut pickled onions in half. Place carrots, cucumbers, pickled onions, tomatoes and peas in a bowl.

3 To make creamy dressing, whisk mayonnaise, yoghurt, mustard, lemon juice, sugar and 3 tablespoons reserved cooking liquid in a bowl. Add salt and pepper to taste.

4 Stir dressing into salad. Distribute among serving bowls. Add lamb's lettuce and alfalfa sprouts.

cook's tip

If lamb's lettuce is not available, use 50g rocket or watercress leaves or a mixture of the two to give this salad a distinctive peppery taste.

Ham salad with grated vegetables

✳ Dice **250g lean ham**. Grate **3 medium carrots**. Peel **1 small celeriac** and grate. Cut **1 thin leek** in half lengthways; slice into narrow strips. Finely dice **4 small gherkins**. Place in a serving bowl.

✳ Whisk **100g whipping cream, 3 tablespoons light soured cream, 1 tablespoon olive oil, 2 tablespoons white wine vinegar, salt** and **freshly ground black pepper** until combined. Stir into salad. Chill, covered, 2 hours. Serve sprinkled with **2 tablespoons finely chopped fresh parsley leaves**.

Mixed salad with ham

Ham, egg and asparagus salad

You can use peeled white asparagus if available, but the green variety is easier to find. Both are an attractive accompaniment for ham and egg, dressed with mayonnaise and yoghurt.

500g white or green asparagus

1 lemon, cut in half

salt

1 teaspoon sugar

350g smoked ham, in one piece

3 tablespoons light mayonnaise

170g yoghurt

1 tablespoon vegetable oil

3 tablespoons chopped fresh chervil
   or flat–leaf parsley

freshly ground black pepper

2 medium eggs, hard–boiled

1 heart cos lettuce

serves 4

preparation 40 minutes

cooking 30 minutes

per serving 228 calories, 11.5g fat, 3g saturated fat,
8g carbohydrate, 7g sugar, 2g fibre, 2.4g salt

1 Trim asparagus and peel if required (see below). Cut into short pieces. Thinly slice one lemon half. Squeeze juice from other half.

2 Bring a large saucepan of salted water to a boil with sugar and lemon slices. Add asparagus. Cook over medium heat, 8 minutes for green and 15 minutes for white, or until crisp-tender. Drain and leave to cool.

3 Trim excess fat from ham. Cut or tear ham into wide strips. Place in a bowl with asparagus.

4 To make dressing, whisk mayonnaise, yoghurt, oil and 1 tablespoon lemon juice in a bowl. Add chervil and salt and pepper to taste. Stir dressing into asparagus and ham.

5 Peel eggs and cut into eighths. Arrange lettuce leaves on individual plates. Add asparagus and ham and garnish with egg slices.

to peel asparagus

1 Wash white or green asparagus and trim the ends.

2 Peel white asparagus from the top, just below spear head, down to the base. Peel a very thin layer from the top and a thicker one at the base.

3 Green asparagus is less woody and seldom requires peeling. If you choose to do so, peel only the lower half.

Chicken with mixed salad greens

To save time, you could use pre-cooked chicken but you won't get the extra taste from the garlic marinade. An appealing touch is the garnish of curled lemon rind.

2 skinless chicken breast fillets (about 300g in total)

1 large clove garlic, crushed

1 head oak leaf lettuce

1 small head frisée lettuce

1 head treviso or round radicchio

2 tablespoons butter

salt and freshly ground black pepper

1 small lemon

3 spring onions, finely sliced

250g button mushrooms, thinly sliced

dressing

125g light soured cream

125g yoghurt

1 tablespoon vegetable oil

1 tablespoon white wine vinegar

1 teaspoon Dijon mustard

salt and freshly ground black pepper

serves 4

preparation + chilling 1 hour 15 minutes

cooking 5 minutes

- -

per serving 240 calories, 14g fat, 7g saturated fat, 6g carbohydrate, 5.5g sugar, 1.5g fibre, 0.4g salt

1 Cut chicken into strips. Place chicken and garlic in a bowl. Stir to combine. Chill, covered, 1 hour. Cut or tear oak leaf lettuce, frisée and radicchio into small pieces. Place in a large bowl.

2 Heat butter in a nonstick pan over medium heat. Cook chicken until golden brown and cooked through, about 5 minutes. Add salt and pepper to taste.

3 To make dressing, whisk soured cream, yoghurt, oil, vinegar and mustard in a bowl until combined. Add salt and pepper to taste. Stir dressing into salad greens. Distribute salad greens among serving plates.

4 Peel thin strips of rind from lemon. Place chicken, spring onions, mushrooms and lemon rind on top of salad greens.

cook's tip

This simple salad is easily varied. Try adding thin strips of pancetta cooked over medium heat in a pan until crisp. Or, sprinkle salad with pine nuts just before serving.

Tarragon chicken salad

The piquant flavour of tarragon is an excellent accompaniment to chicken in both hot and cold dishes. You don't need much as the flavour diffuses quickly through cooked dishes. Oranges and almonds add sweetness and texture.

2 skinless chicken breast fillets (about 300g in total)

350ml chicken or vegetable stock

2 long sprigs tarragon

1 small lemon

3 black peppercorns

2 tablespoons tahini (sesame paste)

salt and freshly ground black pepper

1 medium head chicory

150g baby spinach leaves

2 large oranges, peeled and segmented

45g flaked almonds, toasted

serves 4

preparation 20 minutes

cooking 20 minutes

per serving 250 calories, 12.5g fat, 1.5g saturated fat, 9g carbohydrate, 7.5g sugar, 4g fibre, 0.7g salt

1 Place chicken in a single layer in a shallow pan. Cover with stock. Remove leaves from tarragon sprigs; set aside. Lightly crush stalks with a rolling pin, then add to pan. Using a vegetable peeler, remove a wide strip of rind from lemon. Add to pan with peppercorns.

2 Place pan over moderate heat and bring stock to a boil. Reduce heat to a simmer, cover pan and cook 15 minutes, or until chicken is cooked through. Remove chicken from pan with a slotted spoon; leave to cool. Strain stock and reserve. Discard stalks, rind and peppercorns.

3 To make dressing, whisk tahini with 4 tablespoons reserved stock. Add another 1 to 2 tablespoons if mixture is too thick. Squeeze juice from lemon; stir into dressing. Chop enough tarragon leaves to make 1 tablespoon. Add to dressing. Add salt and pepper to taste.

4 Slice chicory diagonally into narrow pieces. Place on a large serving platter with spinach leaves. Add orange segments and toasted almonds. Slice chicken into wide strips and add to salad. Spoon on dressing.

health guide

Chicken is an excellent source of protein and provides many B vitamins. Removing the skin reduces the fat content considerably, as most of the fat in chicken is found directly beneath the skin.

cook's tip

The combination of tarragon and chicken is a classic. Tarragon has a pronounced aniseed taste. If you are not fond of it, try thyme or rosemary instead.

Chinese chicken salad

Spaghetti or linguine are used instead of noodles, but the soy and ginger dressing gives the salad its Chinese influence. Slice the carrots and peppers into the thinnest strips that you can manage.

250g spaghetti or linguine

2 tablespoons soy sauce

1 tablespoon rice vinegar

3 teaspoons sesame oil

1 teaspoon sugar

1 teaspoon ground ginger

pinch of salt

2 cooked skinless chicken breast fillets (about 300g in total), shredded

2 medium carrots, cut into thin strips

1 medium red pepper, cut into thin strips

2 spring onions, finely sliced

serves 4

preparation 20 minutes

cooking 15 minutes

----

per serving 390 calories, 6.5g fat, 1g saturated fat, 55g carbohydrate, 10g sugar, 4g fibre, 2g salt

cook's tip

Shredded cooked chicken may be marinated in the soy sauce mixture for up to 2 days in the refrigerator. As an alternative, use cooked skinless turkey breast.

1 Cook pasta in plenty of lightly salted boiling water until *al dente*, following package instructions. Drain, rinse under cold running water and leave to cool.

2 Combine soy sauce, vinegar, oil, sugar, ginger and salt in a large bowl. Add chicken, carrots, peppers and spring onions; toss to combine. Add pasta; stir gently to combine.

Chicken salad with avocado

A substantial starter or a light lunch, this chicken-stuffed avocado is packed with flavour and goodness. It's particularly high in good-quality protein.

2 shallots, quartered

125ml dry white wine

4 tablespoons lemon juice

4 black peppercorns

pinch of salt

2 skinless chicken breast fillets (about 300g in total)

2 large avocados

2 small celery stalks

½ cucumber

170g light soured cream

1 tablespoon wholegrain mustard

1 tablespoon sunflower or peanut oil

2 teaspoons white wine vinegar

pinch of sugar

salt and freshly ground black pepper

pinch of cayenne pepper

a few sorrel leaves, optional

serves 4

preparation 15 minutes

cooking 20 minutes

per serving 374 calories, 27g fat, 7g saturated fat, 6g carbohydrate, 4g sugar, 4g fibre, 0.8g salt

1 Place shallots, wine, 1 tablespoon lemon juice, 125ml water, peppercorns and salt in a pan; bring to a boil. Add chicken fillets and return to a boil. Reduce heat to low, cover pan and cook chicken 15 minutes, or until cooked through. Remove pan from heat. Leave chicken to cool in cooking liquid.

2 Halve avocados and remove seeds. Remove 4 teaspoons of flesh from each avocado half. Dice, place in a bowl. Mix with 1 tablespoon lemon juice to prevent browning. Drizzle cut surface of avocado halves with 1 tablespoon lemon juice.

3 Dice celery. Peel cucumber, cut in half lengthways and remove seeds with a small spoon. Dice cucumber. Drain chicken and cut into small cubes. Add chicken, celery and cucumber to diced avocado and stir gently to combine.

4 To make dressing, whisk soured cream, mustard, oil, vinegar, sugar and remaining 1 tablespoon lemon juice in a small bowl. Add salt and pepper to taste. Stir dressing into chicken and vegetables. Spoon mixture into avocado halves.

5 Dust avocados with a little cayenne pepper. Cut sorrel leaves into thin strips, if using, and scatter over avocados. (Sorrel has a distinctive lemony taste.)

Chicken salad with cucumber and watercress

Lightly fry the chicken until it's golden brown on the outside, then place on crisp slices of cucumber and sprigs of peppery watercress dressed with soured cream, yoghurt and chives.

1 sprig rosemary

1 clove garlic, roughly chopped

2 skinless chicken breast fillets (about 300g in total)

2 tablespoons lime juice

salt and freshly ground black pepper

1½ cucumbers

150g watercress

3 tablespoons fresh chervil, finely chopped

3 tablespoons fresh dill, finely chopped

3 tablespoons chives, finely chopped

2 tablespoons sunflower or peanut oil

mustard and lemon dressing

125g light soured cream

125g yoghurt

50ml milk

½ teaspoon tarragon or other herb mustard

1 tablespoon lemon-flavoured olive oil

2 tablespoons lemon juice

salt and freshly ground black pepper

serves 4

preparation + chilling 1 hour 15 minutes

cooking 12 minutes

----

per serving 238 calories, 13g fat, 4g saturated fat, 6g carbohydrate, 5.5g sugar, 1g fibre, 0.3g salt

1 Roughly chop rosemary leaves and combine with garlic in a bowl. Add chicken; turn to coat. Drizzle with lime juice and sprinkle with salt and pepper. Chill, covered, 1 hour.

2 Peel fine strips of skin lengthways from cucumber. Slice cucumbers thinly. Divide watercress into small sprigs.

3 To make mustard and lemon dressing, whisk soured cream, yoghurt, milk, mustard, oil and lemon juice in a large bowl until combined. Add salt and pepper to taste. Add cucumber, watercress and herbs to bowl. Stir to coat completely with dressing.

4 Heat oil in a nonstick frying pan over medium heat. Add chicken and cook, turning occasionally, 8 to 10 minutes, until cooked through. Remove from pan and set aside for a few minutes.

5 Arrange cucumber and watercress salad on individual plates. Cut chicken crossways into thick slices; add to salad.

Chicken and pineapple salad with curry dressing

Pineapple and mandarins or oranges provide a sweet contrast to savoury chicken and celery blended in a light citrus and ginger curry yoghurt.

1 chicken (about 1.6kg)

2 medium onions, roughly chopped

2 celery stalks, roughly chopped

2 medium carrots (about 250g),
    roughly chopped

1 bay leaf

2 teaspoons salt

1 teaspoon whole black peppercorns

½ small sweet pineapple (about 500g)

3 mandarins, tangerines or small oranges

2 thin leeks

heart of 1 cos lettuce

lemon balm leaves, for garnish

curry dressing

4 tablespoons light mayonnaise

125g yoghurt

4 tablespoons orange juice

2 tablespoons lemon juice

2 teaspoons mild curry powder

pinch of ground ginger

pinch of cayenne pepper

salt and freshly ground black pepper

serves 4

preparation 30 minutes

cooking 1 hour 15 minutes

---

per serving 462 calories, 9g fat, 2g saturated fat, 31g carbohydrate, 27g sugar, 6g fibre, 1.1g salt

1 Place chicken, chopped vegetables, bay leaf, salt and peppercorns in a large saucepan. Cover with water. Bring to a boil. Skim off surface with a slotted spoon. Cook, partly covered, over low heat 1 hour 15 minutes. Remove pan from heat. Leave chicken to cool in cooking liquid.

2 Separate chicken meat from carcass and chop flesh into small pieces; place in a bowl.

3 Trim pineapple, discard core and cut fruit into small pieces. Peel and segment 2 mandarins. Add pineapple and mandarin pieces to chicken. Cut leeks in half lengthways and cut into very fine strips. Add to bowl.

4 To make curry dressing, whisk mayonnaise, yoghurt, orange juice and lemon juice until combined. Stir in curry powder, ginger and cayenne pepper. Add salt and pepper to taste. Stir dressing into chicken and pineapple mixture.

5 Peel and slice remaining mandarin crossways. Tear or cut lettuce into wide strips. Distribute among serving bowls and top with chicken salad. Garnish with mandarin slices and lemon balm leaves.

cook's tip

Curry dressing can be varied in several ways. Use 4 tablespoons lime juice in place of orange juice and omit the lemon juice. Or, use hot curry powder and leave out the ginger.

Chicken kebab salad with peanut sauce

Pak choi is the green base for a salad that also includes peppers, bean sprouts and chillies. A peanut dipping sauce for the chicken conjures up an Indonesian satay.

400g kinless chicken breast fillets

small piece fresh ginger

1 clove garlic, crushed

3 tablespoons salt-reduced soy sauce

1 tablespoon lemon juice

3 tablespoons sunflower or peanut oil

½ teaspoon sambal oelek or Chinese
   chilli paste

4 small fresh red chillies

1 medium red pepper

small head baby pak choi

150g mung bean sprouts

2 spring onions, thinly sliced

3 tablespoons lime juice

salt and freshly ground black pepper

peanut sauce

3 tablespoons crunchy or smooth
   peanut butter

1 teaspoon soft brown sugar

1 can (165ml) light coconut milk

1 tablespoon white wine vinegar

2 tablespoons soy sauce

½ teaspoon sambal oelek

serves 4

preparation + chilling 1 hour 30 minutes

cooking 10 minutes

per serving 336 calories, 20g fat, 6g saturated fat, 13g carbohydrate, 11g sugar, 2g fibre, 2.3g salt

1 Cut chicken breast fillets into large cubes. Peel ginger and grate finely. Combine ginger, garlic, soy sauce, lemon juice, 1 tablespoon oil and sambal oelek in a bowl. Add chicken and turn to coat. Chill, covered, 1 hour.

2 To make chilli flowers, using a sharp knife, make 6 cuts from the stem to the tip of each chilli; do not cut through the base (see below right). Place chillies in a bowl of iced water until ready to serve.

3 Halve pepper and cut into thin strips. Cut pak choi into thin strips. Arrange pepper, pak choi, mung beans and spring onions in serving bowls. Whisk lime juice with remaining 2 tablespoons oil. Add salt and pepper to taste. Drizzle over vegetables.

4 Heat grill to medium high. Remove chicken from marinade and thread onto 12 skewers. Cook chicken about 6 minutes, turning occasionally.

5 To make peanut sauce, place all ingredients in a pan over low heat. Cook 5 minutes or until sauce thickens.

6 Place kebabs on top of salad. Coat with peanut sauce, serving remainder separately. Remove chillies from iced water and add to salad.

to make chilli flowers

1 Make 6 cuts in each chilli, from the stem to the tip; do not cut through the base. The chillies should still be intact.

2 Place chillies in iced water. Gradually, the individual strips will curl outwards.

3 Drain chillies. Remove seeds, if wished. Chilli flowers are usually used as a garnish and are not eaten. Warn guests if they are not fond of very hot chillies.

Chicken liver and apple salad

Chicken liver and apple salad

Chicken livers add lots of flavour to all kinds of dishes. Here they are marinated in red wine and fried with apples for a sweet and savoury warm salad.

400g chicken livers

125ml dry red wine

2 tablespoons balsamic vinegar

1 bay leaf

1 sprig thyme

1 small head oak leaf lettuce

3 tablespoons vegetable oil

2 medium onions, sliced into thin rings

2 medium tart apples

1 tablespoon butter

1 tablespoon lemon juice

3 tablespoons dry white wine

pinch of ground aniseed

1 tablespoon sultanas

salt and freshly ground black pepper

serves 4

preparation + chilling 1 hour 30 minutes

cooking 10 minutes

per serving 289 calories, 14g fat, 3.5g saturated fat, 16g carbohydrate, 14g sugar, 2g fibre, 0.3g salt

1 Place chicken livers in a bowl. Add red wine, 1 tablespoon vinegar, bay leaf and thyme. Chill, covered, 1 hour.

2 Tear lettuce into small pieces and arrange on 4 serving plates. Heat 2 tablespoons oil in a nonstick pan. Add onions and fry until golden brown. Remove from pan; keep warm.

3 Peel apples and slice thinly. Heat butter in a saucepan over medium heat, add apple slices and cook briefly. Add lemon juice, wine, ground aniseed and sultanas. Cover pan; cook another 3 minutes or until apples have softened but still hold their shape. Remove from heat.

4 Remove chicken livers from bowl with a slotted spoon, reserving marinade. Pat livers dry on paper towel. Heat remaining 1 tablespoon oil in a nonstick pan over high heat and cook chicken livers on all sides, 2 to 3 minutes. Add salt and pepper to taste. Place chicken livers on top of lettuce.

5 Pour reserved marinade into pan and bring to a boil. Add remaining 1 tablespoon vinegar and salt and pepper to taste. Drizzle over salad. Arrange apples and onions on top.

Warm chicken livers with green beans and tomatoes

✱ Marinate **400g chicken livers** as in main recipe. Trim **500g green beans**; cut into short lengths. Cook in **vegetable stock** to cover, about 10 minutes. Drain and let cool. Dice **1 medium red onion**. Drain **8 oil-packed sun-dried tomato halves** and chop finely.

✱ Mix beans, onions, tomatoes and **1 tablespoon chopped fresh oregano** in a serving bowl. Whisk **2 tablespoons olive oil**, **2 tablespoons balsamic vinegar**, **salt** and **pepper** and pour over salad. Heat **3 tablespoons olive oil** in a nonstick pan. Cook chicken livers 2 to 3 minutes. Add to salad.

Cheese, sausage and potato salad

Turn a potato salad into a main course by adding frankfurters and cheese, along with gherkins, peppers and sweetcorn.

2 thick slices gouda cheese

6 frankfurters, thinly sliced

1 orange and 1 red pepper

3 medium, unpeeled, cooked potatoes

1 can (420g) sweetcorn, drained and rinsed

8 small gherkins in vinegar, thinly sliced

2 tablespoons vegetable oil

2 tablespoons white wine vinegar

2 tablespoons vinegar from jar of gherkins

125g yoghurt

pinch of sugar

¼ teaspoon ground sweet paprika

salt and freshly ground black pepper

30g finely chopped chives

serves 4

preparation 35 minutes

marinating 1 hour

----

per serving 452 calories, 19g fat, 6g saturated fat, 58g carbohydrate, 17g sugar, 5g fibre, 2.3g salt

1 Cut cheese into strips. Place in a bowl with frankfurters. Halve peppers and cut into small cubes. Peel potatoes and cut into small cubes. Add peppers, potatoes, corn and gherkins to bowl and mix well.

2 Whisk oil, white wine vinegar and vinegar from gherkins in a bowl. Stir in yoghurt, sugar and ground paprika. Add salt and pepper to taste. Stir into salad. Chill, covered, 1 hour.

3 Taste salad just before serving. Add more salt and pepper to taste. Sprinkle with chives.

cook's tip

Try to cook potatoes a day ahead; the flavour will be improved. About 400g cooked rice may be used in this salad in place of the potatoes.

Sausage, potato and radish salad

✳ Cut **6 cooked turkey or chicken sausages** into thin rounds and place in a serving bowl. Peel and dice **500g waxy potatoes** cooked the previous day (see cook's tip). Slice **1 small white onion** into thin rings. Cut **12 large red radishes** into quarters. Add potatoes, onions and radishes to bowl.

✳ Whisk **3 tablespoons balsamic vinegar**, **3 tablespoons vegetable oil**, **1 teaspoon wholegrain mustard** and **salt** and **pepper** to taste. Stir into salad. Add **2 tablespoons finely chopped fresh parsley**.

Cheese, sausage and potato salad

Turkey and mushroom salad

You can use turkey escalopes or chicken breasts in this recipe. Stuff large mushrooms with a mix of diced meat, chopped lettuce, pan juices and crème fraiche and serve on a bed of mixed leaves with fresh raspberries.

250g turkey escalopes or chicken breasts

2 tablespoons butter

salt and freshly ground black pepper

12 large white mushrooms

125ml dry white wine

1 bay leaf

1 sprig rosemary

2 tablespoons vegetable oil

3 tablespoons raspberry vinegar

2 tablespoons crème fraîche or
    soured cream

1 head oak leaf lettuce

125g fresh raspberries

serves 6

preparation 10 minutes

cooking 15 minutes

per serving 160 calories, 11g fat, 5g saturated fat, 2g carbohydrate, 1.5g sugar, 1g fibre, 0.5g salt

1 Cut turkey into small pieces. Heat 1 tablespoon butter in a nonstick pan over medium heat. Add turkey; cook 2 to 3 minutes or until golden and cooked through. Season with salt and pepper; transfer to a plate.

2 Wipe mushrooms with kitchen paper. Discard stalks. Heat remaining 1 tablespoon butter in pan over medium heat. Add mushrooms, open side up, and cook 3 minutes. Add wine, bay leaf, rosemary and a generous grinding of pepper. Cook, covered, another 5 minutes.

3 Transfer mushrooms to a plate. Cook pan juices over high heat until reduced to one third their original volume. Discard rosemary and bay leaf. Leave pan juices to cool.

4 Pour pan juices into a large bowl. Whisk in oil, vinegar and crème fraîche. Add salt and pepper to taste. Finely chop 4 lettuce leaves. Add to bowl with turkey; stir to combine.

5 Spread remaining whole lettuce leaves on serving plates. Place mushrooms on top, open sides up, and fill with turkey salad. Garnish with raspberries.

raspberries

Raspberries are an excellent source of vitamin C. They are also high in pectin, a form of soluble fibre that helps control blood cholesterol levels. In addition, they provide bioflavonoids that may protect against cancer.

Turkey and fruit salad

Make an easy, healthy lunch with low-fat strips of turkey served with two varieties of grapes, plusmelon balls and walnuts.

1 small head iceberg lettuce

1 head treviso or round radicchio

1 small cantaloupe or honeydew melon (about 500g)

250g red seedless grapes

250g green seedless grapes

1 tablespoon butter

500g turkey escalopes or turkey breast fillets, cut into thin strips

salt and freshly ground black pepper

1 tablespoon fresh lemon thyme leaves

25g walnuts

dressing

2 tablespoons crème fraîche or soured cream

2 tablespoons walnut oil

3 tablespoons lemon juice

salt and freshly ground black pepper

serves 4

preparation 20 minutes

cooking 10 minutes

per serving 400 calories, 17g fat, 5g saturated fat, 29g carbohydrate, 27g sugar, 2g fibre, 0.5g salt

health guide

Melons contain pectin, a type of soluble fibre that may help keep blood cholesterol levels in check. Melons may also help protect against cardiovascular disease and some cancers.

1 Cut or tear iceberg lettuce and radicchio into small pieces. Arrange on individual serving plates.

2 Halve melon and discard seeds. Scoop out flesh with a melon baller. Cut grapes in half. Scatter melon balls and grapes over salad greens.

3 Heat butter in a nonstick pan over medium heat. Cook turkey until browned and cooked through, about 8 minutes. Season with salt and pepper. Stir in lemon thyme.

4 To make dressing, whisk crème fraîche, oil and lemon juice in a bowl. Add salt and pepper to taste. Drizzle over salad greens. Top with turkey and garnish with walnuts.

Turkey with fruit and nuts

Here's turkey with fruit again – but this time it's smoked turkey breast that's combined with fresh plums and mushrooms in a goat's cheese dressing.

2 tablespoons grapeseed or vegetable oil

3 shallots, finely sliced

150g fresh chanterelle or white mushrooms, finely sliced

3 tablespoons fresh parsley, finely chopped

1 tablespoon lemon juice

salt and freshly ground black pepper

300g smoked turkey breast, sliced

2 small heads treviso or round radicchio

3 ripe but firm plums (about 200g), halved and stoned

25g walnuts

cheese dressing

100g creamy goat's milk cheese

3 to 4 tablespoons milk

1 tablespoon red wine vinegar

salt and freshly ground black pepper

serves 4

preparation 15 minutes

cooking 10 minutes

---

per serving 290 calories, 18g fat, 6g saturated fat, 7g carbohydrate, 6g sugar, 2g fibre, 1g salt

cook's tip

If plums are not in season, use fresh fruits, such as apricots or pears as an alternative. Pecans, blanched almonds or pistachios or a mixture of nuts may be used in place of walnuts.

1 Heat oil in nonstick pan over medium heat. Add shallots; cook until transparent. Add mushrooms; cook 3 minutes, stirring. Add parsley and lemon juice. Season to taste with salt and pepper. Remove from heat. Stir in turkey.

2 Tear or cut radicchio into small pieces and use to line a serving platter. Top with turkey and mushroom mixture. Cut plums into thin slices and add to salad.

3 To make cheese dressing, beat cheese, 3 tablespoons milk and vinegar in a bowl until well combined. If mixture is not sufficiently runny, add remaining 1 tablespoon milk. Add salt and pepper to taste. Drizzle dressing over salad. Garnish with walnuts.

Fish & Seafood Salads

The crunch of salad greens and the succulence of shellfish and fresh or canned fish come together in colourful salads that range from ultra simple to sophisticated. Fish and seafood need little preparation and can be quickly steamed, baked, grilled or poached. They are good for heart health if eaten regularly.

Italian seafood salad

Insalata di mare is a showcase for top-quality seafood.
For maximum flavour, use fresh produce, not frozen.

4 tablespoons lemon juice

125ml white wine vinegar

5 black peppercorns

½ teaspoon fennel seeds

½ teaspoon salt

300g baby squid or calamari,
  gutted and cleaned

1kg mussels, scrubbed and debearded

375ml dry white wine

1 bay leaf

300g medium, cooked prawns, peeled and
  deveined, leaving tails intact

2 celery stalks, thinly sliced

2 plum tomatoes, finely diced

1 medium red onion, finely diced

2 cloves garlic, finely chopped

3 tablespoons fresh flat-leaved parsley,
  finely chopped

heart of 1 cos lettuce

vinaigrette

5 tablespoons olive oil

3 tablespoons lemon juice

pinch of cayenne pepper

salt and freshly ground black pepper

serves 4

preparation 30 minutes

cooking 30 minutes

per serving 420 calories, 18g fat, 3g saturated fat,
8g carbohydrate, 4.5g sugar, 1g fibre, 2.4g salt

1 Bring 500ml water to a boil with lemon juice, vinegar, peppercorns, fennel seeds and salt. Add squid and cook over low heat until tender, about 20 minutes. Leave squid in liquid to cool.

2 Leave mussels in a bowl of cold water for 15 minutes, then strain. Discard open mussels. Rinse remaining mussels in cold water until all traces of sand are removed.

3 In a large saucepan, bring white wine and bay leaf to a boil. Add mussels, cover and cook for about 10 minutes until they open. Strain, and discard any mussels that remain closed. Remove flesh from open shells. Set aside to let cool.

4 Remove squid from cooking liquid and cut into small pieces. Combine squid, mussels and prawns in a bowl. Mix in celery, tomatoes, onion, garlic and parsley. Place lettuce leaves on individual bowls or plates.

5 To make vinaigrette, whisk oil, lemon juice and cayenne pepper until combined; add salt and pepper to taste. Drizzle over salad, toss lightly and spoon onto lettuce.

mussels

Choose mussels that are firmly closed or that close when tapped sharply or squeezed. Any open mussels must be discarded as they are not fit for eating.

White fish salad with olive vinaigrette

Most kinds of white fish will work with this salad. Use sustainable species if you can. Serve cool with artichokes and tomatoes.

500g hake or other firm white fish fillets

1 tablespoon olive oil

½ teaspoon black peppercorns

1 sprig rosemary, 2 sprigs oregano,
    2 sprigs thyme and 1 bay leaf tied in
    a bunch

1 small lemon, thinly sliced

3 large tomatoes

6 marinated artichoke hearts

4 tablespoons fresh flat-leaved parsley,
    finely chopped

olive vinaigrette

1 tablespoon olive oil

1 tablespoon balsamic vinegar

1 tablespoon lemon juice

2 cloves garlic, finely chopped

15 pitted green olives and 15 pitted
    black olives, finely chopped

½ teaspoon dried thyme

½ teaspoon dried oregano

salt and freshly ground black pepper

serves 4

preparation 35 minutes

cooking 5 to 8 minutes

----

per serving 236 calories, 14g fat, 1.5g saturated fat,
4g carbohydrate, 3g sugar, 1g fibre, 0.8g salt

1 Cut fish fillets into small pieces. Brush a steamer basket with oil and add fish. Place peppercorns, bunch of herbs and lemon slices in a large saucepan.

2 Pour in water to a depth of about two fingers, taking care water does not touch fish in steamer basket. Insert steamer basket and bring water to a boil. Cover fish and cook 5 to 8 minutes, depending on its thickness. Remove steamer basket from saucepan and let fish pieces cool in it.

3 Halve tomatoes, remove seeds and slice into rounds. Cut artichokes into small pieces. Arrange tomatoes, artichokes, parsley and fish pieces on a large platter.

4 To make olive vinaigrette, whisk oil, vinegar, lemon juice and garlic until combined. Fold in olives and herbs; add salt and pepper to taste. Drizzle over salad.

cook's tip

For maximum flavour, marinate the fish pieces in the vinaigrette for up to 2 hours. Then combine with the rest of the ingredients.

White fish salad with olive vinaigrette

White fish salad with fennel and sun-dried tomatoes

✱ Cut **500g firm white fish fillets** into pieces and cook as for main recipe. Slice **2 small fennel bulbs** finely and arrange on a platter. Spread fish on top. Sprinkle with **1 teaspoon fennel seeds**.

✱ Drain **8 sun-dried tomato halves** in oil, chop finely and sprinkle over salad. Whisk **2 tablespoons lemon juice** with **4 tablespoons olive oil** and drizzle over salad. Sprinkle with **salt** and **coarsely ground pepper**.

Tabbouleh with fish in lemon dressing

The bulgur wheat and parsley combination that is tabbouleh is usually served as a side dish or accompaniment, but with the addition of chunks of white fish, it becomes a healthy main course.

180g bulgur wheat

300g white fish fillets

1 small lemon, thinly sliced

2 sprigs parsley

5 black peppercorns

1 medium cucumber, seeds removed, diced

4 spring onions, thinly sliced

250g cherry tomatoes, halved

2 tablespoons fresh coriander, chopped

2 tablespoons fresh mint, chopped

2 tablespoons fresh parsley, chopped

mint sprigs, for garnish

lemon dressing

2 tablespoons olive oil

2 tablespoons red wine vinegar

2 tablespoons lemon juice

1 tablespoon grated lemon peel

1 teaspoon Dijon mustard

1 clove garlic, crushed

salt and freshly ground black pepper

serves 4

preparation + standing 1 hour

cooking 5 minutes

chilling 1 to 2 hours

per serving 294 calories, 7g fat, 1g saturated fat, 38g carbohydrate, 4g sugar, 1g fibre, 0.2g salt

1 Place bulgur wheat in a large heatproof bowl and add 500ml boiling water. Let stand 45 minutes, or until grains are tender and water has been absorbed.

2 Meanwhile, place fish fillets in a large pan, add lemon slices, parsley sprigs and peppercorns and cold water to cover. Bring to a boil. Reduce heat and simmer, covered, 5 minutes, or until fish is opaque and flakes easily.

3 Remove fish from liquid and set aside to cool. Use a fork to separate fish into large flakes.

4 Place bulgur wheat in a serving bowl and add cucumber, spring onions, tomatoes and chopped herbs. Gently mix in fish, taking care not to break it up.

5 To make lemon dressing, whisk all ingredients in a bowl. Pour dressing over salad and mix gently to combine.

6 Chill salad, covered, 1 to 2 hours to allow flavours to develop. Check seasoning before serving and garnish with mint sprigs.

Vietnamese fish salad

It's the peanuts, chillies and rice vinegar that give the salad its Vietnamese flavour. Eat with chopsticks for an authentic Far Eastern experience.

500g white fish fillets, skinned

500ml rice vinegar

2 medium onions, finely sliced

1 tablespoon white sugar

1 teaspoon salt

2 tablespoons raw peanuts, shelled

2 tablespoons white rice

2 tablespoons finely shredded fresh mint

1 fresh red chilli, seeded and finely chopped

extra shredded fresh mint leaves and thin
     slivers of red chilli, for garnish

serves 4

preparation + marinating 1 hour 40 minutes

cooking 5 to 7 minutes

---

per serving 214 calories, 4.5g fat, 1g saturated fat,
15g carbohydrate, 7g sugar, 1g fibre, 1.5g salt

1 Remove small bones from fish; cut fillets in half crossways and slice into long, thin strips. Place in a large bowl with about 300ml rice vinegar, making sure fish is covered with liquid. Marinate 1 hour.

2 Place onions, sugar, salt and remaining vinegar in a bowl. Stir until sugar and salt have dissolved. Leave to soak 30 minutes.

3 Crush peanuts finely. Dry-fry in a heavy nonstick pan over low heat 2 to 3 minutes until evenly browned. Remove from pan and set aside.

4 Add rice to pan and toast 3 to 4 minutes until golden brown all over, then crush finely.

5 Remove marinated fish and onion from vinegar. Place in a large bowl and add mint and chilli. Toss gently to combine; sprinkle toasted crushed peanuts and rice on top and toss again. Garnish with extra mint and chilli.

Tuna and green bean salad

Canned tuna is easiest to find, but if you can get fresh tuna it will work well lightly grilled and then sliced. You can use most kinds of beans, but thin French beans are particularly good in this recipe.

3 cloves garlic, peeled

250g green beans, halved

6 small red potatoes (about 375g), halved

2 tablespoons balsamic or red wine vinegar

2 tablespoons low-fat mayonnaise

1 tablespoon olive oil

pinch of salt

30g fresh basil leaves

250g cherry tomatoes, halved

1 can (425g) water-packed tuna, drained

6 cos lettuce leaves

50g black olives, for garnish

serves 4

preparation 15 minutes

cooking 20 minutes

per serving 281 calories, 8g fat, 1g saturated fat, 22g carbohydrate, 6g sugar, 3.5g fibre, 1g salt

1 Blanch garlic in a large saucepan of boiling water for 3 minutes. Transfer garlic to a food processor or blender; set aside. Add beans to boiling water and cook 4 minutes, or until crisp-tender. Remove beans, rinse under cold water and drain. Add potatoes to pan and cook 12 minutes, or until tender; drain.

2 Add vinegar, mayonnaise, oil and salt to garlic in food processor and purée. Add basil and 2 tablespoons water and purée again.

3 Transfer dressing to a large bowl. Add tomatoes, beans, potatoes and tuna, tossing to coat. Tear lettuce into small pieces. Add lettuce and toss again. Garnish with olives.

tuna

Remarkably lean for a fish with so much flavour, tuna provides good amounts of healthy omega-3 fatty acids. It is also an excellent source of some B vitamins.

Tuna and roasted pepper salad

Tuna and roasted pepper salad

The richness of the tuna is complemented by the smoky sweetness of roasted red and yellow peppers and the crispness of fresh green lettuce.

2 red and 2 yellow peppers

1 clove garlic

1 large head green lettuce, such as lollo bionda

4 tablespoons olive oil

2 tablespoons white balsamic vinegar

salt and freshly ground black pepper

1 can (180g) tuna in water, drained

1 tablespoon small capers

1 tablespoon lemon juice

125g soured cream

1 tablespoon coarsely chopped fresh parsley, for garnish

serves 4

preparation 30 minutes

cooking 15 minutes

per serving 272 calories, 18g fat, 5g saturated fat, 13g carbohydrate, 12g sugar, 3g fibre, 0.4g salt

1 Heat oven to 240°C / gas 9. Place whole peppers on aluminium foil on baking tray. Roast 15 minutes, turning halfway through, or until blackened and blistered.

2 Remove peppers from oven. Place tea towel soaked in cold water on top. Leave 5 minutes. Peel away skin. Cut into broad strips.

3 Cut garlic in half horizontally and rub cut surface over inside of salad bowl. Tear lettuce into small pieces. Add peppers and lettuce to bowl.

4 To make vinaigrette, whisk 2 tablespoons oil with vinegar until combined; add salt and pepper to taste.

5 Using a fork, break tuna into small pieces in a bowl. Add capers. Whisk remaining 2 tablespoons oil, lemon juice, soured cream and salt and pepper to taste and stir into tuna.

6 Drizzle vinaigrette on pepper strips and lettuce. Place on a platter. Add tuna mixture and sprinkle with parsley.

Smoked trout and roasted pepper salad

✳ Prepare **peppers** as for main recipe. Mix with vinaigrette and arrange on a platter. Peel **4 large hard-boiled eggs**, quarter and add to platter. Cut **200g smoked trout** into strips.

✳ Combine **100g crème fraîche** or **light soured cream, 3 tablespoons yoghurt, 2 tablespoons lemon juice** and **herb salt** and **pepper** to taste. Stir in smoked trout and **1 tablespoon finely chopped fresh parsley**. Spoon trout mixture over salad.

Vegetable salad with tuna

This salad combines frozen and fresh ingredients and gives you a good few of your suggested 'five a day' vegetables. When in season, use mangetout in place of frozen peas.

150g frozen peas

150g frozen green beans

salt

3 chilled cooked potatoes (waxy variety), unpeeled

1 yellow and 1 green pepper

1 medium white onion

2 large tomatoes

100g green olives stuffed with pimiento

1 small clove garlic, finely chopped

4 tablespoons mayonnaise

1 tablespoon olive oil

2 tablespoons lemon juice

freshly ground black pepper

1 can (180g) water-packed tuna, drained

lemon wedges, to serve

serves 4

preparation 35 to 40 minutes

cooking 15 minutes

per serving 380 calories, 19g fat, 3g saturated fat, 36g carbohydrate, 10g sugar, 8g fibre, 1.1g salt

1 Bring 125ml water to a boil in a saucepan with ½ teaspoon salt. Add frozen peas and beans, cover and cook 5 minutes. Pour into strainer, reserving liquid. Drain vegetables and let cool.

2 Peel potatoes and cut into small cubes. Trim peppers and cut into short strips. Slice onion into rings. Halve tomatoes, remove seeds and cut into eighths.

3 Halve olives if desired. Place olives, peas, beans, pepper strips, onion rings, tomato wedges and diced potatoes in a serving bowl.

4 Combine garlic, mayonnaise, oil, lemon juice and 3 tablespoons of reserved vegetable cooking water. Stir together until smooth. Add salt and pepper to taste.

5 Pour mayonnaise mixture over vegetables. Flake tuna a little. Arrange on vegetables. Serve with lemon wedges.

green beans

Green beans are low in fat, high in dietary fibre and a good source of B vitamins. If using fresh green beans instead of frozen, remove stems, add to a large saucepan of boiling salted water and cook, uncovered, 4 to 6 minutes, until crisp-tender.

Diced vegetables with tuna

❋ Dice **1 red pepper** and **1 yellow pepper**, **3 large tomatoes**, **1 cucumber**, **2 medium carrots** and **2 large celery stalks**. Arrange on a platter.

❋ Finely dice **1 medium white onion**. Drain and flake **1 can (180g) tuna** in water or olive oil. Combine with onion. Whisk **2 tablespoons mayonnaise**, **125g yoghurt**, **1 tablespoon sunflower oil** and **herb salt** and **pepper** to taste. Stir into tuna and onion mixture. Spoon mixture onto vegetables. Sprinkle with **chopped fresh parsley**.

Tuna and egg salad

Tuna and egg salad

Canned tuna and egg are a classic salad combination and the sliced onion adds crunch while pimento stuffed olives provide extra colour and taste.

2 medium eggs, hard–boiled

2 medium red peppers

50g green olives, stuffed with pimiento

1 large onion

1 small head butterhead lettuce

1 can (425g) tuna in oil, drained

few sprigs oregano, for garnish

herb vinaigrette

4 tablespoons olive oil

3 tablespoons sherry vinegar

1 clove garlic, crushed

salt and freshly ground black pepper

1 tablespoon each fresh thyme, oregano
   and flat–leaved parsley, chopped

serves 4

preparation 30 minutes

per serving 390 calories, 26g fat, 4.5g saturated fat, 8g carbohydrate, 6g sugar, 2g fibre, 1.1g salt

1 Peel hard-boiled eggs and slice into rounds. Dice peppers. Slice olives. Cut onion into thin rings. Separate lettuce leaves and use to line serving plates.

2 Arrange eggs, peppers, onion rings and olives on lettuce leaves. Flake tuna into chunks and add to salad.

3 To make herb vinaigrette, whisk oil, vinegar, garlic and salt and pepper to taste. Stir in chopped herbs.

4 Drizzle vinaigrette over salad. Garnish salad with oregano sprigs.

Tuna salad with peas and onions

✳ Cook **150g frozen peas** in **150ml vegetable stock**. Drain and place in a bowl. Cut **1 medium white onion** into small cubes. Drain **1 can (425g) water-packed tuna** and flake finely. Add onion, tuna and **2 teaspoons small capers** to peas.

✳ To make dressing, stir **4 tablespoons mayonnaise** and **3 tablespoons yoghurt** until smooth. Season with **salt, white pepper, 1 teaspoon dried Italian herbs** and **1 to 2 tablespoons lemon juice**. Mix dressing into salad. Arrange salad in small bowls or pile onto slices of **pumpernickel bread**.

Salmon salad with peas and dill

The lightest touch is needed when cooking this ultra simple but attractive and nutritious salad of salmon fillets on a bed of peas.

400g salmon fillet

1 lemon

200ml fish stock

125ml dry white wine

salt and freshly ground black pepper

200g frozen peas

150ml vegetable stock

1 small head iceberg lettuce

125g light mayonnaise

125g soured cream

1 teaspoon medium to hot mustard

pinch of sugar

2 tablespoons fresh dill, finely chopped

4 dill sprigs, for garnish

serves 4

preparation 30 minutes

cooking 8 to 12 minutes

per serving 395 calories, 27g fat, 7g saturated fat, 8g carbohydrate, 5g sugar, 3g fibre, 0.9g salt

1 Slice salmon into small pieces. Cut 4 thin slices from the lemon. Place fish stock, wine, salt, pepper and lemon slices in a saucepan and bring to a boil.

2 Add fish pieces, cover and cook over low heat 3 to 4 minutes. Remove from pan and let cool. Reserve liquid.

3 Place peas and stock in a small saucepan and bring to a boil. Cook peas 3 to 5 minutes; do not overcook. Drain and let cool.

4 Tear lettuce leaves into small pieces and divide among serving plates. Beat mayonnaise, soured cream, mustard, sugar, salt and pepper with 4 tablespoons fish liquid in a bowl until creamy. Stir in chopped dill.

5 Arrange salmon and peas on lettuce. Drizzle with dressing. Cut remaining lemon into thin slices. Garnish salad with lemon slices and dill sprigs.

cook's tip

When buying salmon fillets, always check that the flesh is moist and shiny and bounces back when pressed. It should have a pleasant sea smell with no browning around the edges.

dill

Fresh dill lifts the flavour of salmon and other seafood. It is also a good complement to eggs, cucumber and potatoes.

Salmon salad with peas and dill

Salmon on lettuce and watercress

✳ Cook **400g salmon** as for main recipe and let cool. Tear leaves of **1 small head of frisée lettuce** into pieces. Separate **100g watercress** into sprigs. Distribute among individual serving plates. Add salmon. Finely dice **1 medium red onion** and sprinkle on top.

✳ Combine **125g soured cream**, **1 tablespoon mayonnaise**, **1 teaspoon Dijon mustard** and **salt** and **pepper** to taste. Fold in **1 tablespoon finely chopped pickled vegetables** and spoon over salad.

Smoked salmon on mixed salad greens

Salmon tartare on vegetable carpaccio

✳ Peel **1 cooked beetroot** and **2 cooked potatoes** and slice thinly. Thinly slice **2 large cooked carrots** and **2 large tomatoes**. Place vegetable slices on individual plates. Sprinkle with **salt** and **pepper**, drizzle with **2 tablespoons rapeseed or groundnut oil** and **2 tablespoons sherry vinegar**.

✳ Finely dice **400g smoked salmon** and place in a bowl. Mix in **2 to 3 tablespoons lemon juice, salt, ground white pepper** and **2 tablespoons finely chopped fresh dill**. Arrange salmon tartare on top of vegetable carpaccio.

Smoked salmon on mixed salad greens

Salmon roe, also known as red caviar, adds a salty richness to this dish. For an extra touch of pure luxury, or for a special occasion, use beluga caviar instead.

1 small head treviso or round radicchio

1 small head frisée lettuce heart

75g watercress leaves

3 tablespoons fresh flat–leaved parsley, finely chopped

400g smoked salmon, thinly sliced

2 tablespoons red caviar (salmon roe)

vinaigrette

4 tablespoons olive oil

4 tablespoons lemon juice

2 tablespoons lime juice

salt and freshly ground white pepper

serves 4

preparation 20 minutes

per serving 261 calories, 16g fat, 2.5g saturated fat, 1g carbohydrate, 1g sugar, 1g fibre, 3.9g salt

1 Cut or tear treviso and frisée leaves into pieces. Arrange salad greens with watercress leaves on individual plates. Sprinkle parsley over the top.

2 Separate salmon slices and cut into small strips. Arrange salmon and caviar on top of salad greens.

3 To make vinaigrette, whisk oil, lemon juice and lime juice until combined; add salt and pepper to taste. Drizzle vinaigrette over salad.

smoked salmon

Smoked salmon has slightly lower amounts of omega-3 fatty acids than fresh salmon, but, like other oily fish, it provides a rich source of these essential nutrients.

cook's tip

Ideally, use freshly smoked salmon for the best result, but if you do use salmon that's vacuum-packed, make sure to check the use–by or best–before date.

Trout fillets with asparagus and tomato salad

Depending on the quantities, this dish makes a sumptuous starter or a light lunch. Smoked trout is delicious but you could use mackerel instead.

1kg medium to thick asparagus spears

1 teaspoon sugar

150g cherry tomatoes, halved

400g smoked trout fillets

4 small eggs, hard–boiled

4 tablespoons sunflower oil

2 tablespoons herb vinegar

1 tablespoon lemon juice

½ teaspoon grated horseradish, from a jar

salt and freshly ground black pepper

4 tablespoons soured cream

1 tablespoon red caviar (salmon roe)

2 tablespoons chopped fresh chives,
   for garnish

serves 4

preparation 30 minutes

cooking 20 to 25 minutes

per serving 424 calories, 27g fat, 7g saturated fat,
8g carbohydrate, 7g sugar, 5g fibre, 2.5g salt

1 Trim ends from asparagus spears. Peel at ends if necessary. Bring plenty of lightly salted water to a boil with sugar. Cook spears for 5 to 10 minutes. Drain; let cool.

2 Arrange asparagus and cherry tomatoes on individual plates. Cut trout fillets into large pieces and add to plates. Peel eggs; cut into quarters.

3 Whisk oil, herb vinegar, lemon juice and horseradish until combined; add salt and pepper to taste. Drizzle over salad and trout.

4 Stir soured cream, season with salt and pepper. Spoon onto each salad portion. Garnish with caviar, eggs and chives.

Japanese-style trout with wasabi and rocket

✳ Finely chop **2 spring onions**. Coarsely grate **200g white radish**. Arrange **150g rocket** on individual serving plates. Top with spring onions and radish. Whisk **2 tablespoons olive oil** and **2 tablespoons lemon juice** until combined; add **salt** and **pepper** to taste. Drizzle over salad.

✳ Remove bones from **300g fresh trout fillets** and chop finely. Mix **1 pinch powered wasabi** with **1 teaspoon rice vinegar**, **1 tablespoon Japanese rice wine** and **1 pinch ground ginger**; add **salt** and **pepper** to taste. Combine with trout. Add to salad. Garnish each serving with a little **caviar**.

Trout fillets with asparagus and tomato salad

Herring salad with citrus fruit

Oily herrings get a wonderful flavour contrast when served with chunks of juicy fresh orange and lemon in a citrus vinaigrette.

2 large oranges

2 large lemons

3 spring onions

250g herring fillets in oil, drained

fresh lemon balm leaves, for garnish

citrus vinaigrette

3 tablespoons sunflower oil

50ml orange juice, freshly squeezed

2 tablespoons lemon juice

1 tablespoon white wine vinegar

salt and freshly ground mixed peppercorns

serves 4

preparation 35 minutes

marinating 2 hours

per serving 275 calories, 17.5g fat, 2.3g saturated fat, 13g carbohydrate, 12g sugar, 2g fibre, 0.7g salt

1 With a sharp knife, remove skin and white pith from oranges and lemons. Working over a bowl, separate oranges and lemons into segments and set aside. Reserve juice.

2 Thinly slice spring onions. Set aside a few light green rings for garnish.

3 Cut herring fillets into small pieces and arrange on a platter with citrus segments and spring onions.

4 To make citrus vinaigrette, whisk oil, reserved juice, orange juice, lemon juice and vinegar until combined; add salt and pepper to taste. Drizzle over salad. Cover and refrigerate at least 2 hours to allow flavours to develop.

5 Remove salad from refrigerator and stand until at room temperature. Garnish with spring onion rings and lemon balm. Serve with pumpernickel or dark wholegrain bread.

Prawn and mango salad

Sweet and soft fleshed, mangoes go well with all kinds of fish and meat including the king prawns used here. They're dressed with lime juice, chilli and mint.

½ medium cucumber

1 medium red pepper, sliced

250g cherry tomatoes, quartered

2 large mangoes, peeled and sliced

16 cooked king prawns, peeled and deveined, leaving tails intact

150g mixed salad leaves

1 clove garlic, crushed

1 tablespoon chilli sauce

2 tablespoons olive oil

4 tablespoons lime juice

3 tablespoons fresh mint, chopped

freshly ground black pepper

serves 4

preparation 25 minutes

----

per serving 175 calories, 7g fat, 1g saturated fat, 21g carbohydrate, 19g sugar, 4.5g fibre, 0.9g salt

1 Slice cucumber into thin rounds, leaving skin on. Combine cucumber, pepper, tomatoes, mangoes, prawns and salad leaves in a large bowl.

2 To make dressing, combine garlic, chilli sauce, oil, lime juice and mint in a small screw-top jar. Shake well. Stir dressing into salad.

3 Pile salad onto individual serving plates. Season with freshly ground pepper to taste.

cook's tip

Mangoes are an excellent source of the antioxidant beta carotene. If fresh mangoes are not available, substitute avocado slices for an equally nutritious salad.

Seafood salad with saffron and parsley

Meaty textured swordfish and prawns are quick-cooked with garlic and saffron and a touch of wine. The remaining juice is combined with sherry vinegar for the dressing.

1 red and 1 yellow pepper

1 cos lettuce

250g swordfish steaks

2 tablespoons lemon juice

salt and freshly ground black pepper

5 tablespoons olive oil

12 uncooked king prawns, peeled and deveined, tails intact

3 cloves garlic, cut into fine slices

¼ teaspoon ground saffron

150ml dry white wine

2 tablespoons sherry vinegar

4 sprigs curly-leaved parsley, for garnish

serves 4

preparation 30 minutes

cooking 10 minutes

per serving 270 calories, 17g fat, 3g saturated fat, 5g carbohydrate, 5g sugar, 1.5g fibre, 0.4g salt

1 Cut peppers into strips. Cut or tear lettuce leaves into strips. Place lettuce and pepper on individual plates.

2 Cut swordfish into small pieces. Drizzle with lemon juice; sprinkle with salt and pepper.

3 Heat 3 tablespoons oil in a nonstick frying pan. Sear fish pieces and prawns on all sides over medium-high heat. Add garlic and saffron and fry briefly. Add wine. Cook, uncovered, until wine is reduced by half.

4 Using a slotted spoon, lift fish and prawns from liquid and place on salad. Remove pan from heat and season pan juices with salt, pepper and sherry vinegar. Drizzle over salad.

5 Heat remaining 2 tablespoons oil in a small, heavy pan. Lightly brown parsley over medium heat. Remove, drain briefly on kitchen paper and arrange on salad.

Crisp seafood salad with yoghurt dressing

Crisp, crunchy iceberg lettuce with creamy yoghurt and sweet baby prawns make an ideal combination for a summertime salad.

1 medium head iceberg lettuce

50g sorrel or baby spinach leaves

250g cherry tomatoes

150g cooked and peeled prawns, thawed if frozen

4 sprigs dill, for garnish

4 thin lemon slices, for garnish

vinaigrette

2 tablespoons rapeseed or olive oil

2 tablespoons lemon juice

salt and ground white pepper

yoghurt dressing

250g yoghurt

2 tablespoons mayonnaise

1 teaspoon dry vermouth

1 tablespoon lime juice

salt and ground white pepper

pinch of cayenne pepper

serves 4

preparation 30 minutes

per serving 210 calories, 14g fat, 3g saturated fat, 8g carbohydrate, 7g sugar, 1g fibre, 0.9g salt

1 Cut lettuce into strips. Tear larger sorrel leaves into pieces. Arrange lettuce and sorrel on serving plates. Cut tomatoes into quarters and add to salad.

2 To make vinaigrette, whisk oil and lemon juice until combined; add salt and pepper to taste. Drizzle over lettuce.

3 To make yoghurt dressing, stir yoghurt, mayonnaise, vermouth and lime juice until creamy. Season well with salt, white pepper and cayenne pepper.

4 Spoon yoghurt dressing and prawns on to salad. Garnish with dill and lemon slices.

cook's tip

In place of dry vermouth in the yoghurt dressing, use 1 teaspoon dry white wine or 1 teaspoon orange juice. Dry vermouth has a slightly 'herby' taste and aroma.

Iceberg lettuce with salmon

✳ Finely shred **1 medium head iceberg lettuce**. Slice **3 celery stalks** into thin strips and finely grate **2 medium carrots**. Combine in a serving bowl.

✳ Whisk **2 tablespoons olive oil**, **3 tablespoons lemon juice**, **1 teaspoon wholegrain mustard**, **¼ teaspoon sugar** until combined; add **salt** and **white pepper** to taste. Pour over salad and stir to combine.

✳ Cut **100g smoked salmon** into strips and place on top of salad. Garnish with lemon slices and celery leaves.

Crisp seafood salad with yoghurt dressing

Crab and grapefruit salad

White crabmeat is sweet and succulent with a flaky texture. Buying pre-picked crabmeat will save a lot of preparation time. It contrasts well with the sharpness of grapefruit and the slightly bitter chicory.

4 medium grapefruit

2 tablespoons mayonnaise

1 tablespoon mango chutney, finely chopped

2 teaspoons Dijon mustard

1 teaspoon sesame oil

salt and freshly ground black pepper

400g crabmeat, picked over to remove any
    pieces of shell or cartilage

1 head chicory, cut crossways into thin strips

100g watercress, tough stems trimmed

1 head soft lettuce, such as mignonette,
    separated into leaves, for serving

serves 4

preparation 25 minutes

per serving 262 calories, 13g fat, 2g saturated fat,
14g carbohydrate, 13g sugar, 3g fibre, 1.5g salt

1 Remove skin and white pith from grapefruit with a paring knife. Working over a bowl, separate grapefruit segments from membranes; reserve juice.

2 Whisk mayonnaise, chutney, mustard, sesame oil, a pinch of salt and pepper and 3 tablespoons reserved grapefruit juice in a medium bowl.

3 Dice crab and stir into mayonnaise mixture. Add chicory, watercress and grapefruit segments and toss to combine. Serve crab salad on a bed of lettuce leaves.

grapefruit

Chemical compounds in this citrus fruit cause the body to absorb more of certain drugs, which can result in receiving a larger dose than intended. This effect is not seen with other citrus juices.
Avoid taking any medication with grapefruit juice. Grapefruit is rich in pectin, a type of dietary fibre that seems to reduce low-density lipoprotein cholesterol.

Crab salad with papaya

Fresh crab has a rich flavour that works well with the taste of papaya. Select whole papaya with a fragrant aroma.

4 medium cooked crabs (400g each)

2 spring onions

150g canned hearts of palm, drained

2 celery stalks

1 medium ripe papaya or pawpaw

3 tablespoons sunflower oil

3 tablespoons lime juice

3 tablespoons fish stock

2 teaspoons Dijon mustard

salt and freshly ground black pepper

pinch of soft brown sugar

pinch of cayenne pepper

3 tablespoons fresh flat-leaved parsley,
    finely chopped

2 sprigs mint

lime slices, for garnish

serves 4

preparation 40 minutes

- -

per serving 290 calories, 16g fat, 2g saturated fat,
7g carbohydrate, 6g sugar, 2g fibre, 1.8g salt

1 Remove crabmeat from the claws and legs of crabs, then remove meat and entrails from the bodies. Discard entrails, keeping only the livers.

2 Cut crabmeat and livers into pieces. Cut undersides of shells along the curved join and break off. Rinse out shells with warm water and let dry.

3 Thinly slice spring onions. Cut hearts of palm into small cubes. Cut celery stalks into small cubes. Halve papaya and scrape out seeds; peel and cut flesh into small cubes. Mix crab pieces and salad ingredients together in a bowl.

4 To make vinaigrette, whisk oil, 2 tablespoons lime juice, fish stock, mustard, salt, pepper, sugar and cayenne pepper until combined. Finely chop mint leaves. Add mint and parsley.

5 Drizzle vinaigrette on salad ingredients. Season with salt, cayenne pepper and remaining 1 tablespoon lime juice. Spoon into crab shells. Garnish with lime slices.

breaking open and shelling crabs

1 First carefully twist the claws and legs of the crab away from the shells and break off.

2 Using lobster shears or a nutcracker, crack open the claws. Remove meat by pulling it out of the legs using a lobster fork.

3 Lift the tail plates on the undersides of the crab; remove with a twisting movement. Lift out the meat and entrails.

per serving 449 calories, 19g fat, 4g saturated fat, 24g carbohydrate, 8g sugar, 3.5g fibre, 1.7g salt

in a nonstick pan and lightly fry bread cubes over medium heat, turning often and taking care that they do not burn. Spoon salad into bowls, top with rocket and croutons.

Scallops and grapefruit with mustard vinaigrette

Scallops, like most seafood, need light, gentle cooking or they tend to become rubbery. Their delicate flavour is offset by the not-too-sweet, not-too-sour flavour of grapefruit.

1 medium red onion

½ head frisée lettuce

100g rocket

2 medium pink grapefruit

12 shelled scallops with coral

2 tablespoons lemon juice

salt and freshly ground black pepper

1 tablespoon butter

2 tablespoons dry vermouth

mustard vinaigrette

3 tablespoons olive oil

2 tablespoons red wine vinegar

1 teaspoon wholegrain mustard

1 teaspoon honey

salt and freshly ground black pepper

serves 4

preparation 20 minutes

cooking 5 minutes

per serving 231 calories, 13g fat, 3.5g saturated fat, 12g carbohydrate, 9g sugar, 2g fibre, 0.4g salt

1 Finely dice onion. Tear lettuce into bite-size pieces. Remove hard stems from rocket.

2 With a sharp knife, remove skin and white pith from grapefruit. Separate grapefruit into segments.

3 Drizzle scallops with lemon juice and sprinkle with salt and pepper. Heat butter in a nonstick pan and cook scallops about 2 minutes on each side; add vermouth and cook another 1 to 2 minutes. Remove from heat.

4 To make vinaigrette, whisk oil, vinegar, mustard and honey until thickened slightly; add salt and pepper to taste.

5 Arrange lettuce leaves on individual plates and drizzle with vinaigrette. Top with diced onion and grapefruit segments. Arrange scallops on top.

scallops

The muscle from the large white scallop shells is particularly firm, but still tender. It has a mild, slightly sweet taste. A scallop shell also cntains a roe sack, the orange-red coral, that is prized by gourmets. Scallops are a good source of zinc and provide iron.

Grilled calamari with tomato vinaigrette

Marinade slices of squid in oil, wine and parsley for two hours, then cook briefly. Serve with a dressing made with tomatoes and champagne vinegar. If you don't have champagne, use white wine vinegar instead.

500g calamari or squid rings

2 cloves garlic, crushed

4 tablespoons fresh flat-leaved parsley, finely chopped

2 tablespoons olive oil

4 tablespoons white wine

salt and freshly ground black pepper

1 small head cos (romaine) lettuce

tomato vinaigrette

2 large tomatoes

2 tablespoons olive oil

1 tablespoon champagne vinegar

2 tablespoons lemon juice

4 sprigs fresh thyme, finely chopped

salt and freshly ground pepper

serves 4

preparation + marinating 2 hours 30 minutes

cooking 3 minutes

----

per serving 223 calories, 13g fat, 2g saturated fat, 4g carbohydrate, 2g sugar, 0.7g fibre, 0.4g salt

1 Place calamari, garlic and parsley in a bowl. Add oil, wine, salt and pepper. Mix together, cover and marinate in refrigerator about 2 hours.

2 Tear lettuce into pieces and arrange on individual plates. Halve tomatoes, remove seeds and finely dice.

3 To make tomato vinaigrette, whisk oil, champagne vinegar, lemon juice and thyme until combined; add salt and pepper to taste. Add diced tomatoes and mix together. Drizzle vinaigrette over lettuce leaves.

4 Heat grill to medium heat. Cook calamari under grill about 3 minutes, turning occasionally. Place on salad and serve while hot.

cook's tip

Calamari is also delicious when cooked on a barbecue. Sear until just cooked through and make sure the rings don't turn black or the flesh will taste bitter.

Grilled calamari with tomato vinaigrette

Grilled calamari salad

✳ Marinate and grill **500g calamari or squid rings** as for main recipe. Tear **1 lollo rossa lettuce** into bite-size pieces. Thinly slice **1 medium red onion**. Arrange lettuce leaves and onion rings on a platter.

✳ Finely chop **3 red peppers** and **2 cloves garlic**. In a blender, purée peppers and garlic; blend in **3 tablespoons olive oil**, **2 tablespoons lemon juice**, salt, pepper and cayenne pepper. Pour over salad. Arrange calamari on top.

Dessert Fruit Salads

Fresh fruit salads, with their refreshing flavours and vibrant colours, make the perfect finale to a meal. Keep salads simple or indulge a little with toppings such as fruit purées, chopped nuts, praline and cream or chocolate sauces. In winter, when there is less choice, dried fruit and canned fruit are useful options.

Fruit & berries at a glance

Fruit and berries are perhaps the best ingredients for desserts and puddings – here, in a range of inspired fruit salads. They also often add an extra, unexpected element to savoury salads, both those with meat and fish and vegetable dishes. Try to eat at least two servings of fresh fruit every day for long-term good health.

shopping

As a general rule, the heavier the fruit, the juicier it is and the better it will taste; and the stronger the scent of a fruit, the riper it will be. The flesh of a ripe, perfect piece of fruit should yield to a light touch. Spots or signs of mould indicate that the fruit is spoiled. Buy fruit in season and buy only as much fresh fruit as you will eat in the next two days. Fully ripe fruit can only be stored for a limited time. Buy quick-ripening fruit, such as pears or bananas, at different levels of ripeness so that they don't all have to be eaten at the same time.

storing

Wash fruit thoroughly just before eating. Store any delicate varieties, such as melons, berries, apricots and peaches, in the vegetable crisper of the refrigerator. Apples, hard pears, citrus fruit, firm peaches and nectarines can be stored at room temperature as they are harvested unripe and continue to ripen during storage. Berries and grapes, on the other hand, should be eaten quickly, because they are harvested when ripe and soon become rotten. They keep for a few days in the refrigerator. Do not squash berries as bruising will cause the delicate fruit to spoil rapidly. Note that unripe fruit ripens more quickly if a ripe piece of fruit is stored with it, or if the fruit is stored in a brown paper bag at room temperature.

nutrition

Most fruit is fat-free, has a high water content and contains few calories. Depending on the variety,

fresh fruit also contains abundant nutrients, such as vitamin C and folic acid, as well as numerous minerals and trace elements. Fruit and berries are also rich in carotenoids as well as bioflavonoids, phytochemicals and fibre. Apples and pears should not be peeled, or peeled only thinly, because the majority of vitamin C and other nutrients are found in and under the skin.

how much per person

For fruit salad, allow 150g to 250g of peeled, trimmed fruit per serving, depending on the dressing you are using. Allow a little more fruit for light yoghurts, dressings or marinades. For richer cream dressings, 150g will be enough. A small, hollowed-out melon or pineapple half filled with fruit salad is enough for one serving.

bananas

Bananas don't grow on trees but on giant herbs related to the lily and orchid family. They continue to ripen after picking. When buying, select a range at different stages of ripeness so they won't all ripen at once. Look for shiny yellow skins, either unblemished or with just a few brown spots. Bananas are high in vitamin C and contain a mix of carbohydrates that provide sustained energy. They are also a good source of dietary fibre, potassium and vitamin B$_6$.

berries

Smaller berries often have more flavour than large ones. Always rinse berries briefly in cold water, then trim only if necessary. Delicate varieties such as raspberries, strawberries and blackberries should be used on the day that they are picked, if possible. The more robust varieties will keep in the refrigerator for up to 2 days. The simplest of berry dessert salads can be made by adding sugar to berries and serving them with yogurt or, for something special, zabaglione.

grapes

Classed as berries, most varieties of purple/red and green grapes grown for eating are sweet and juicy with a high glucose and fructose content. Select plump, well-coloured grapes, firmly attached to their stems. Avoid soft or wrinkled fruit and those browning around the stem. Grapes are generally picked when ripe and sweet, to be eaten fresh. Store grapes, unwashed, in the refrigerator in a sealed container or plastic bag. Use within 2 to 3 days.

mangoes

The orange-coloured flesh of the mango is sweet, fragrant and succulent and it has fibrous but edible strands surrounding the very large seed. Select firm, bright mangoes that have a distinct pleasant aroma. Let ripen at room temperature. Store ripe fruit in the vegetable crisper or in a plastic bag in the refrigerator. Use within 3 days.

melons

Melons such as galia melons, muskmelons, cantaloupes and rockmelons should smell aromatic without any hint of acetone. They should have no soft spots or cracks and certainly no mould formation. Ripe specimens yield slightly to pressure at the stems. They do not ripen further after harvesting and will only get softer. Ripe watermelons have firm red flesh and brown seeds. When buying watermelons, test them for ripeness by tapping the melon and listening carefully. If it sounds firm and echoes, it is ripe. If it sounds dull, it has been picked for some time or is unripe. Store uncut melons at room temperature. Once cut, cover and refrigerate. Melons add a refreshing note to summer salads.

pineapples

Pineapple flesh contains a protein-splitting enzyme, so fresh pineapple tastes sour with milk products and prevents gelatine from setting. This enzyme is destroyed by heating and it can tenderise meat if used in a marinade. Select plump pineapples with a sweet, pleasant aroma and fresh-looking skin and leaves. Pineapples do not ripen further after picking. They become juicier, but not sweeter, once harvested. Store in a cool place. Once cut, cover and refrigerate. Use within 2 days.

stone fruits

Fully ripe plums and peaches are juicy and sweet and the stones are easy to remove. Firm, less ripe plums and peaches are often tart and are just as suitable for salads or eating raw. The flesh of ripe peaches and plums yields to gentle pressure. Purée ripe, juicy peaches and serve as a fruit sauce with fruit salad.

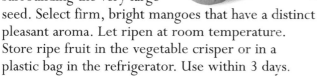

Berry salad with mascarpone cream

Strawberries, blueberries, blackberries and redcurrants are sweetened with a little lemon juice and icing sugar and served with crumbs of sponge and mascarpone cream flavoured with orange liqueur.

250g each blueberries, blackberries
   and redcurrants

250g strawberries

4 tablespoons icing sugar

2 tablespoons lemon juice

10 sponge finger biscuits

mascarpone cream

200g mascarpone

2 tablespoons milk

2 tablespoons orange liqueur or orange juice

1 tablespoon sugar

icing sugar, for dusting

serves 4

preparation 20 minutes

per serving 466 calories, 22g fat, 14g saturated fat, 52g carbohydrate, 49g sugar, 6g fibre, 0.15g salt

1 Combine all the berries in a bowl. Mix icing sugar and lemon juice and pour over berries. Stir carefully to combine.

2 Place sponge fingers in a plastic bag. Seal and place on a flat surface. Crush with a rolling pin to make coarse crumbs. Spread crumbs on dessert plates. Top with berries.

3 To make mascarpone cream, whisk mascarpone, milk, orange liqueur and sugar in a bowl until thick and well combined. Spoon a little mascarpone cream onto each serving. Dust with a little icing sugar.

cook's tip

Try a combination of peaches, apricots, plums and mangoes and flavour the mascarpone cream with almond liqueur instead of orange.

Berry salad with pistachio cream

✳ Mix **250g blueberries**, **250g raspberries** and **250g redcurrants** in a large bowl. Cut **350g strawberries** into halves and add to bowl. Combine **4 tablespoons crème de cassis liqueur**, **1 tablespoon lemon juice** and **3 tablespoons icing sugar**. Pour over berries and stir gently to combine. Spoon into dessert bowls.

✳ To make pistachio cream, whip **125g double cream** with **1 tablespoon vanilla sugar** until thickened. Finely grind **3 tablespoons chopped pistachios** in a food processor. Fold into cream. Serve with berries.

Berry salad with mascarpone cream

Kiwifruit and blueberry salad

The colour and pattern of kiwis makes an elegant background for blueberries and almond slivers. Drizzle with raspberry cream laced with liqueur and vanilla.

55g flaked almonds

8 kiwifruit

125ml port or red wine

few small strips lemon peel

250g blueberries

icing sugar, for garnish

raspberry cream

150g frozen raspberries, thawed

4 tablespoons icing sugar

2 teaspoons vanilla sugar

2 tablespoons raspberry liqueur
   or almond liqueur

125g double cream

serves 4

preparation 15 minutes

cooking 5 minutes

----

per serving 485 calories, 25g fat, 11g saturated fat, 42g carbohydrate, 42g sugar, 5g fibre, trace salt

1 Dry roast flaked almonds in a pan over medium heat until golden, tossing to prevent burning. Transfer to a plate and leave to cool. Peel kiwifruit and slice crossways.

2 Place port and lemon peel in a pan. Bring to a boil; add kiwifruit. Reduce heat to low. Poach fruit 1 minute. Remove pan from heat. Remove fruit with a slotted spoon, discarding lemon peel, and leave to cool. Arrange on serving plates with blueberries.

3 To make raspberry cream, place raspberries in a fine sieve over a bowl. Press berries with the back of a spoon to make a fine purée without any seeds. Reserve a little purée for decoration. Stir icing sugar, vanilla sugar and raspberry liqueur into purée. Fold in cream.

4 Dust kiwifruit and blueberries with icing sugar. Spoon a little raspberry cream onto plates. Using a teaspoon, swirl in a little reserved purée. Scatter on roasted flaked almonds.

Blackberry and lychee salad with yoghurt

Lychees are widely available these days and add an exotic touch to peaches and blackberries. The yoghurt dressing is enhanced with amaretti biscuits and vanilla sugar.

2 tablespoons flaked almonds

2 ripe peaches

1 tablespoon lemon juice

250g blackberries

1 can (560g) lychees, drained

125ml orange juice, freshly squeezed

3 tablespoons dry marsala or sherry

pinch of ground mace

2 teaspoons icing sugar

50g small amaretti biscuits

250g yoghurt

2 teaspoons vanilla sugar

mint or lemon balm leaves, for garnish

serves 4

preparation 20 minutes

per serving 322 calories, 9.5g fat, 1.5g saturated fat, 47g carbohydrate, 47g sugar, 4g fibre, 0.1g salt

cook's tip

To make vanilla sugar, push a dried vanilla bean into a jar of sugar. After about two weeks, take it out. The vanilla flavour and aroma will have permeated the sugar.

1 Dry roast flaked almonds in a pan over medium heat until golden, tossing to prevent burning. Transfer to a plate.

2 Halve peaches and cut into slices. Place in a bowl; drizzle with lemon juice to prevent discolouration. Add blackberries and lychees. Combine orange juice, marsala, ground mace and icing sugar in a bowl. Drizzle mixture over fruit. Place mixture in serving bowls.

3 Place amaretti biscuits in a plastic bag. Seal, place on a flat surface and crush with a rolling pin to make fine crumbs. Combine yoghurt, vanilla sugar and amaretti crumbs. Spoon over fruit. Add flaked almonds and mint leaves.

Mixed fruit salad in melon halves

Small round cantaloupe melons were first cultivated near Cantalupo in Italy, during the mid-18th century. Turn them into fruity bowls and fill with cherries, bananas, apricots and plums.

250g sweet cherries

1 medium banana

4 apricots

250g damsons or other blue plums

3 tablespoons lemon juice

4 tablespoons liquid honey

3 sprigs mint

2 small cantaloupe or honeydew melons

125g double cream

mint leaves, for garnish

serves 4

preparation 30 minutes

---

per serving 321 calories, 13g fat, 8g saturated fat, 50g carbohydrate, 47g sugar, 4g fibre, 0.2g salt

1 Remove stones from cherries. Slice banana, apricots and plums. Combine fruit in a bowl.

2 Mix lemon juice and honey and pour over fruit. Remove mint leaves from sprigs. Cut into fine strips. Stir into salad.

3 Halve melons and scrape out seeds. Use a melon baller to scoop out flesh, leaving a rim of flesh about 1cm thick. Add melon balls to bowl.

4 Whip cream until stiff. Spoon fruit salad into melon halves. Garnish with cream rosettes and mint leaves.

cook's tip

Prepare the melons ahead of time and keep covered in the refrigerator. Any mixture of seasonal fruit may be used in this recipe.

cherries

The flavour and low-calorie content of the various sweet cherry varieties (more than 1000 worldwide) make cherries an ideal snack. Sour cherries are more nutritious than the sweet types. They are available dried and can be used in jams and jellies.

variety of different fruit in season such as strawberries or blackberries with an exotic fruit like Cape gooseberries (in picture).

3 Whisk orange juice, maple syrup and rum and stir into salad. Place pineapple halves on dessert plates and fill with fruit salad. Drizzle with chocolate topping and sprinkle roasted flaked almonds on top.

Make a refreshing summer dessert

to make caramel

1 Place sugar cubes, lemon juice and water in a heavy-based saucepan with a heat-proof handle. Bring to a boil over high heat until sugar has dissolved.

2 Boil uncovered until large bubbles form and syrup reaches about 140°C. Do not stir, or the sugar will crystallise and be unsuitable for use. Do not let sugar burn.

3 Push bubbles aside with a wooden spoon, carefully watching colour. As soon as sugar is an amber colour, remove from heat and finish as described in main recipe.

Pineapple salad with almond brittle

You need only use plain yoghurt for the yoghurt cream that accompanies the pineapple and almond brittle. It will get a strong citrus flavour from the orange juice, peel and liqueur.

sunflower oil, for brushing

50g sugar cubes (about 12 cubes)

1 teaspoon lemon juice

1 to 2 teaspoons ground cinnamon

100g flaked almonds

1 medium pineapple (about 2kg)

2 tablespoons brown sugar

orange peel and mint leaves, for garnish

yoghurt cream

125g yoghurt

50ml freshly squeezed orange juice

½ teaspoon orange peel, finely grated

1 tablespoon orange liqueur

1 teaspoon icing sugar

125g double cream

serves 4

preparation 40 minutes

cooking 8 to 10 minutes

per serving 604 calories, 29g fat, 10g saturated fat, 79g carbohydrate, 75g sugar, 8g fibre, 0.1g salt

1 To make almond brittle, brush a piece of baking parchment with oil; set aside. Place sugar cubes, lemon juice and 3 tablespoons water in a heavy saucepan with a heat-proof handle; cook until caramelised (see opposite).

2 Remove saucepan from heat. Immediately stir cinnamon and flaked almonds into the caramel; spread mixture onto prepared baking parchment, keeping almond flakes as far apart as possible. Let brittle cool.

3 Heat oven to 220°C / gas 7. Peel pineapple and cut into slices. Arrange slices on ovenproof dessert plates and sprinkle with brown sugar. Bake 8 to 10 minutes and remove. Let cool until lukewarm.

4 To make yoghurt cream, stir yoghurt, orange juice, orange peel, orange liqueur and icing sugar together until smooth and creamy. Whip cream until stiff and fold into yoghurt mixture.

5 Chop cooled almond brittle or crush coarsely with a rolling pin. Spoon yoghurt cream into the centre of each salad portion and sprinkle almond brittle on top. Garnish with orange peel and mint leaves. Serve while lukewarm.

Citrus fruit salad with chocolate

Very simple, but good-looking enough for an 'occasion' dessert: pink grapefruit, orange, and tangerines are marinated in a special liqueur and served with pretty swirls of dark and white chocolate.

50g white chocolate

50g dark chocolate

3 large pink grapefruit

2 large oranges

4 large mandarins or tangerines

2 tablespoons lemon juice

1 tablespoon lime juice

2 tablespoons orange liqueur

2 tablespoons maple syrup or honey

icing sugar, for dusting

1 teaspoon each of lime and orange peel

serves 4

preparation + marinating 1 hour

per serving 271 calories, 8g fat, 4.5g saturated fat, 47g carbohydrate, 44g sugar, 5g fibre, trace salt

1 Melt white and dark chocolate separately in double-boilers. Pour each into a plastic bag and cut a very tiny corner from each bag. Pipe decorative spirals of white and dark chocolate onto dessert plates and chill in refrigerator.

2 Peel grapefruit, oranges and mandarins, removing white pith. Separate into segments and place on a platter.

3 Mix lemon juice, lime juice, orange liqueur and maple syrup. Pour over fruit, cover and marinate 30 minutes in refrigerator for flavours to develop.

4 Arrange fruit on prepared dessert plates and dust with icing sugar. Top with peel, and serve while still well chilled.

Orange and figs with sherry cream

Set the freshest figs on thin slices of blood and standard oranges, then add a dollop of sherry cream with added maple syrup and lemon juice.

2 medium oranges

2 medium blood oranges

6 ripe figs

3 tablespoons pistachios, coarsely chopped

sherry cream

3 tablespoons double cream or crème fraîche

4 tablespoons cream sherry

1 tablespoon maple syrup or honey

1 tablespoon lemon juice

1 small pinch of ground cloves

125g whipping cream

serves 4

preparation 20 minutes

per serving 360 calories, 24g fat, 12g saturated fat, 25g carbohydrate, 24g sugar, 4g fibre, trace salt

1 Using a zester or sharp knife, slice off thin strips of orange peel; set aside. Peel oranges and blood oranges, removing white pith. Cut into slices and arrange on plates.

2 Thinly peel figs if necessary. Cut into quarters and arrange decoratively on plates.

3 To make sherry cream, combine double cream, sherry, maple syrup or honey and lemon juice in a bowl and beat well. Add ground cloves.

4 Whip cream until stiff. Gently fold into sherry mixture. Spoon dollops of sherry cream over fruit portions. Sprinkle with strips of orange peel and pistachios.

figs

To peel soft ripe figs, cut off the stalk ends and carefully peel off the skin, leaving as much flesh as possible.

Mango and papaya salad with cranberries

Packed with all kinds of beneficial vitamins and other nutrients, mango and papaya are elegantly displayed with cranberries in a special red wine and brandy sauce.

2 fully ripe mangoes

1 fully ripe papaya or pawpaw

2 tablespoons lime juice

1 medium tart apple

1 medium orange

1 tablespoon unsalted butter

150g fresh or frozen cranberries

160ml port or red wine

250ml brandy

1 tablespoon honey

2 cloves

½ cinnamon stick

serves 4

preparation 20 minutes

cooking 10 minutes

per serving 350 calories, 3.5g fat, 2g saturated fat, 34g carbohydrate, 32g sugar, 6g fibre, trace salt

1 Peel mangoes and slice. Halve papayas, remove black seeds; peel and slice. Arrange papaya and mango slices alternately on a large platter; drizzle with lime juice.

2 To make cranberry sauce, peel apple and dice. Halve orange. Cut thin strips of orange peel from one half, then squeeze both halves.

3 Heat butter in a saucepan and sauté diced apples until butter begins to brown. Add cranberries, orange peel, port, brandy, orange juice, honey and spices, and bring to a boil. Reduce, uncovered, over medium heat for 5 minutes. Remove from heat.

4 Remove orange peel and spices from sauce. Pour sauce over salad while hot.

Orange and pomegranate salad with vanilla cream

Saturate orange segments in a mix of orange juice, grenadine syrup and lime juice, then serve with pomegranate seeds and a vanilla and rose-flavoured cream.

6 large juicy oranges
4 tablespoons grenadine syrup
2 tablespoons lime juice
1 pomegranate
¼ teaspoon lime peel, grated
125g whipping cream
250g vanilla ice cream
2 teaspoons rose water
icing sugar, for dusting

serves 4
preparation 30 minutes

---

per serving 360 calories, 19g fat, 12g saturated fat, 36g carbohydrate, 34g sugar, 4g fibre, 0.14g salt

1 Peel oranges, removing white pith. Reserve juice. Separate into segments and arrange on plates.

2 Combine reserved orange juice, grenadine syrup and lime juice and pour over orange segments.

3 Cut out crown of pomegranate, then break pomegranate apart. Take out seeds, removing inner white skins. Sprinkle seeds and grated lime peel over orange segments.

4 Whip cream until stiff. Add ice cream and quickly blend with a hand blender until creamy. Spoon onto each salad portion. Drizzle with rose water. Dust with icing sugar.

Warm summer fruit
salad with sabayon

Warm summer fruit

Spiced seasonal fruit salad

This recipe is easily adapted to showcase other summer fruits and berries, including peaches and raspberries. Mustard and cayenne pepper give a subtle spicy heat while coconut adds an appealing texture to the unusual dressing.

1 large mango, peeled and sliced

250g cherries, pitted

100g seedless green grapes

250g strawberries, hulled and cut in half

3 large apricots, halved, stoned, sliced

55g desiccated coconut

1 tablespoon caster sugar

generous pinch of cayenne pepper

generous pinch of mustard powder

pinch of salt

serves 6

preparation 20 minutes

chilling 2 hours or overnight

per serving 138 calories, 6g fat, 5g saturated fat, 21g carbohydrate, 20g sugar, 4g fibre, 0.1g salt

1 Place all the fruit in a large serving bowl.

2 Finely grind coconut in a spice mill or with a pestle and mortar. Add remaining ingredients and mix well.

3 Add spiced coconut mixture to fruit and stir well to combine. Cover and refrigerate at least 2 hours, preferably overnight to allow the flavours to blend and develop.

cook's tip

Canned fruit may be used in this recipe. If you do substite canned for fresh, drain thoroughly to remove as much of the syrup as possible and halve the amount of sugar in the spiced coconut mixture.

mix and match

* Replace apricots with **2 large peaches or nectarines** or **3 large plums**.

* If cherries are out of season or expensive, use a mixture of **seedless green, black and red grapes**. You will need **300g** in total.

* Stir **4 or 5 small, very thin pieces of lemon peel** into the fruit salad before refrigerating.

Vanilla rhubarb with strawberries

Rhubarb pieces are briefly cooked then chilled. Then they're served with strawberries in a superb sauce made with puréed strawberries, orange liqueur and white wine.

800g thin rhubarb stalks

1 vanilla bean

160ml dry white wine

3 to 4 tablespoons sugar

500g strawberries

2 tablespoons orange liqueur

1 tablespoon icing sugar

serves 4

preparation + chilling 1 hour 10 minutes

cooking 10 minutes

----

per serving 153 calories, 0.3g fat, 0g saturated fat, 28g carbohydrate, 27g sugar, 4g fibre, trace salt

1 Peel rhubarb stalks and cut into small pieces.

2 Split open vanilla bean lengthways and scrape out seeds. Cut in half crossways. Place rhubarb, vanilla pod, vanilla seeds, wine and sugar in a saucepan and bring to a boil.

3 Cook rhubarb, covered, over low heat 4 to 5 minutes. The pieces should still hold their shape and not become very soft. Remove from heat, let rhubarb cool. Refrigerate 1 hour.

4 Remove vanilla bean and spoon rhubarb into small bowls. Cut about two thirds of the strawberries into pieces and place in food processor with orange liqueur and icing sugar. Purée until a strawberry froth forms on the surface.

5 Pour puréed strawberries over rhubarb pieces. Garnish with remaining strawberries.

Dried fruit salad

A range of dried fruits is briefly cooked with vanilla to soften them and add flavour, then served with orange flower water and yoghurt on the side.

225g pitted prunes

135g dried apricots

125g dried peaches or pears, halved

55g sultanas

few thin strips orange peel

1 vanilla bean, halved

100g sugar

2 tablespoons orange flower water
  or rose water

250g low-fat yoghurt, to serve

serves 6

preparation + chilling 1 hour

cooking 25 minutes

per serving 262 calories, 1g fat, 0.3g saturated fat, 62g carbohydrate, 60g sugar, 6g fibre, 0.1g salt

1 Place prunes, apricots, peaches, sultanas and orange peel strips in a large saucepan with 1 litre water. Scrape seeds from vanilla bean; add seeds and bean to pan. Partly cover and bring slowly to a boil.

2 Cover and simmer 5 minutes. Add sugar and stir until dissolved. Cover and simmer over low heat a further 15 minutes; allow to cool.

3 Drain, transfer to a serving bowl with a little juice from the pan. Stir in orange flower water. Refrigerate, covered, 1 hour. Serve with yoghurt on the side.

orange flower water

Orange flower water is a natural extract made from the distillation of orange blossoms. It has a delicate fragrance and an intense flavour. It is used in Middle Eastern and Mediterranean dishes, particularly desserts.

Contributors

Super Salads was edited and produced by the Reader's Digest Association Limited, London

Editor Lisa Thomas

Art Editor Julie Bennett

Designer Martin Bennett

Nutritionist Fiona Hunter

Photographers Christiane Kruger, Ian Hoffstetter, Sian Irvine, assisted by Joe Giacomet

Food stylist John Bentham

Proofreader Adèle Linderholm

Indexer Diane Harriman

READER'S DIGEST GENERAL BOOKS

Editorial Director Julian Browne

Art Director Anne-Marie Bulat

Managing Editor Nina Hathway

Head of Book Development Sarah Bloxham

Picture Resource Manager Sarah Stewart Richardson

Pre-Press Technical Manager Dean Russell

Product Production Manager Claudette Bramble

Senior Production Controller Katherine Tibbals

Colour origination by FMG

Printed and bound in China

Super Salads was adapted from *Tolle Salate* published by Reader's Digest, Germany in 2005 and is published by The Reader's Digest Association Limited, 11 Westferry Circus, Canary Wharf, London E14 4HE

We are committed both to the quality of our products and the service we provide to our customers. We value your comments, so please so contact us on 08705 113366 or via our website at www.readersdigest.co.uk

If you have any comments or suggestions about the content of our books, email us at gbeditorial@readersdigest.co.uk

Concept code:	US4499/G
Book code:	400-486 UP0000-1
ISBN:	978 0 276 44638 2
Oracle code:	250007128H.00.24